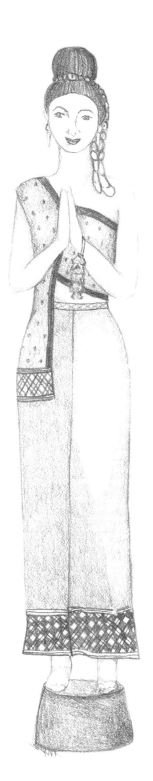

TASTE OF LAOS

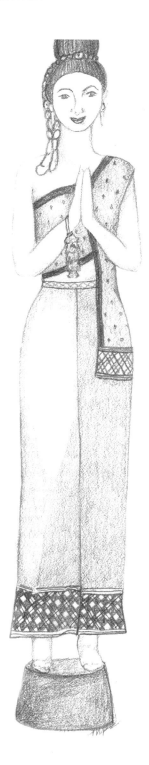

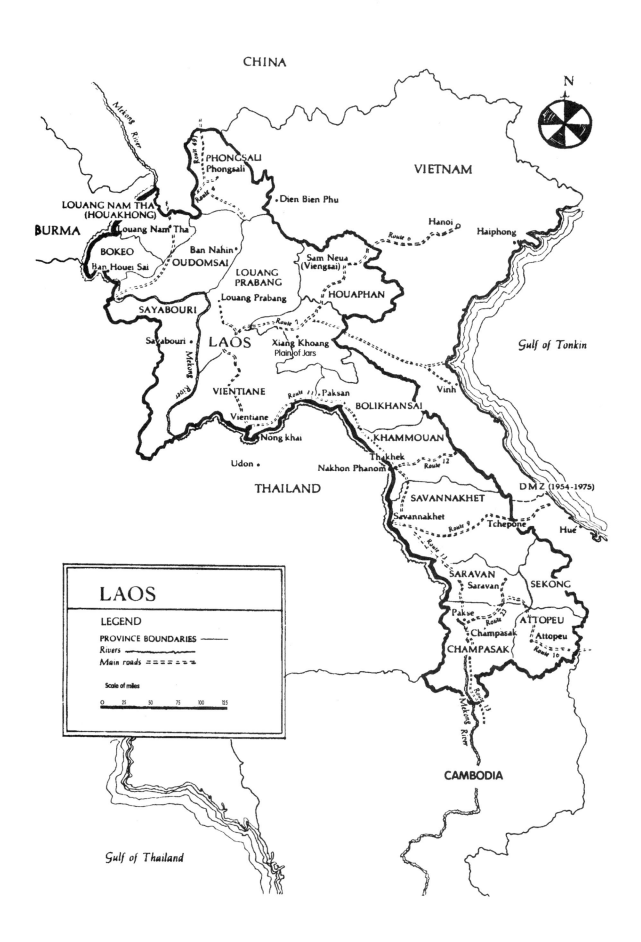

CHINA

VIETNAM

BURMA

N

Mekong River

Route 69

PHONGSALI
Phongsali

LOUANG NAM THA
(HOUAKHONG)

Louang Nam Tha

BOKEO

Ban Houei Sai

Ban Nahin

OUDOMSAI

• Dien Bien Phu

Sam Neua
(Viengsai)

Route 6

Hanoi

Haiphong

LOUANG
PRABANG

SAYABOURI

Louang Prabang

HOUAPHAN

Gulf of Tonkin

Sayabouri •

LAOS

Route 7

Xiang Khoang
Plain of Jars

VIENTIANE

Route 11 • Paksan

Mekong River

Vientiane

BOLIKHANSAI

Vinh

Nong khai

KHAMMOUAN

Udon •

Thakhek
Nakhon Phanom

Route 12

DMZ (1954-1975)

THAILAND

SAVANNAKHET

Savannakhet

Route 9

Tchepone

Hué

Route 11

SARAVAN

Saravan

SEKONG

Pakse

Route 23

ATTOPEU

Champasak

Attopeu

CHAMPASAK

Route 10

Mekong River

Route 13

CAMBODIA

Gulf of Thailand

LAOS

LEGEND

PROVINCE BOUNDARIES ———
Rivers ———
Main roads = = = = = =

Scale of miles

0   25   50   75   100   125

TASTE OF LAOS
LAO/THAI RECIPES
FROM DARA RESTAURANT

By
Daovone Xayavong

ຊິມອາຫານລາວ
ຕຳອາຫານການລັບດານາ
ຊຸມໂດຍ
ດາວວນໄຊຍະວົ້ງ

SLG BOOKS
Berkeley/Hong Kong

SLG Books
P.O. Box 9465
Berkeley, California 94709
USA
Tel: 510-525-1134
Fax: 510-525-2632
E-mail: lao@slgbooks.com
URL: www.slgbooks.com

Color separations and printing by
Snow Lion Graphics, Berkeley/ Hong Kong

Library of Congress Cataloging-in-Publication Data

Xayaong, Daovone, 1960
    Taste of Laos : Lao/Thai recipes from Dara Reataurant / by Daovone Xayavong : editor, Roger Williams ; foreword by Alan Davidson.
        p. cm.
    ISBN 0-943389-32-1
    1. Cookery, Lao. 2. Cookery, Thai. 3. Dara Restaurant. I. Williams, Roger, 1946- II Title.

TX724.5.L28 X39 2000
641.59594—dc21   00-039045

10 9 8 7 6 5 4 3 2 1
First Published June 2000
Printed in Hong Kong

TABLE OF CONTENTS

STEAMED STICKY RICE

STICKY RICE KABOBS

PREFACE

It's not often that the publishers of a book take the opportunity to address the reader. We would like to personally welcome you, dear reader, to the last undiscovered cuisine of Southeast Asia

The easy to follow recipes in this original cookbook will appeal not only to those of you who already have acquired a fondness for Thai food but also to those adventurous diners among you looking for new ways to titillate your taste buds. Its similarity to Thai food makes it familiar to Thai food lovers; its use of different herbs and sauces will make it an appealing addition to the long list of Asian cuisines we have taken as our own.

A few words about the structure of the book itself seem in order here.

1. There is an extensive glossary at the back of *Taste of Laos*. Please refer to it if you have any questions about the exotic ingredients used in some of the recipes.

2. Many of the recipes call for a dipping sauce. For easy reference these have all been included in the "Dipping Sauce" section. I encourage you to make the sauce first, before you prepare the recipe in which it is used.

3. Just in case you would like to try your hand at making your own chili or curry pastes, you will find the recipes and instructions in the "Curry Pastes" section

4. You should use your own judgement when it comes to the amount of chilies to be used in each of the recipes.

5. The original recipes measure cilantro by the number of plants used. Most of you will only find cilantro sold in bunches. For the sake of convenience I have listed the quantity as the number of stalks needed. If cilantro is being used as a garnish then the quantities are not so important.

6. Attention vegetarians: almost all of the recipes that call for meat will become authentic vegetarian dishes if you substitute tofu, in any of its myriad incarnations, or gluten. Please remember to replace fish sauce with soy sauce where appropriate.

7. Most of the recipes have a short paragraph before the list of ingredients that will tell you something about either the preparation or the origin of the dish.

8. Included in this book are recipes for "Ant Egg and Tamarind Soup" and "Young Banana Tree Soup." Both are popular dishes in Laos. Even though they might not appeal to the western palate these dishes are very much a part of Lao food culture. John Bear won't admit to partaking of the Ant Egg and Tamarind Soup but I did. It is really quite good. Tangy and full of protein, it tastes much better than it imagines.

9. Alan Davidson instructs us in his foreword not to worry about those details that would not worry the Lao. Although authenticity was our goal don't pass over a recipe just because you can't find cilantro root.

To the readers as yet unfamiliar with Lao food we say, "Be daring and try the catfish salad or the fresh rolls to start."

Roger Williams
Publishers, SLG Books
Berkeley, California
March 23, 2000

A WORD ABOUT LAO FOOD

Southeast Asian cuisine is essentially a combination of Indian and Chinese cooking styles. Incorporating local ingredients and traditional recipes result in the contemporary cuisine of each of the regions. Certain Laotian and Thai dishes pre-date the influence from Chinese or Indian cuisine.

A good example is vegetarian cooking which is firmly rooted in the Buddhist tradition. In the past, most Lao became vegetarians purely for religion reasons. With the religious restrictions on meat consumption the preparation of vegetables such as cabbage, broccoli, tofu, and bamboo shoots along with the seasonings sesame oil, garlic, green onions, pepper, cilantro and mint make Lao vegetarian dishes similar to Chinese vegetarian food.

The very popular and well-known coconut milk and turmeric curries from Laos and Thailand show the culinary influence from India.

Using local herbs from Laos and Thailand we have adapted and modified our chili pastes to produce a variety of curries such as red curry, green curry, yellow curry, penang curry, and massaman curry which are some of the world's truly great tastes.

In Lao cuisine, we offer an enormous range of dishes with a subtle blend of flavors. Although Lao people generally prefer hot, spicy food not all dishes are equally fiery. Lao food is never bland and it can be modified to please most palates.

For food lovers, Lao food is a treat offering almost endless possibilities for discovering exciting new tastes, rich in quality and variety. The country possesses an abundance of vegetables and fruits, herbs and spices, succulent seafood and fresh farm produce all of which are wonderfully combined to produce a seemingly unlimited number of recipes that make up the repertoire of Lao culinary art. This abundance and variety of ingredients, along with different methods of preparation promise that no matter how often you dine on Lao food there is always a fresh, delicious taste discovery to be made. Our creativity in cooking is not only because of our love of good food but also the result of the wealth of ingredients available to us.

In this book we combine both Thai and Lao food. The secret to success with these recipes is to maintain a delicate balance between Thai spices and Lao herbs mixed with the main ingredients. Remember presentation is as important a part of the culinary cultural history of Laos as the delicious taste of the fresh ingredients.

One food that does set Laos apart from most of Asia is its preference for sticky rice. Sticky rice, *kao neaw*, which originated in Laos, has been the staple for family–style eating in Laos for a long time. It is said, "Laos – sticky rice. Thailand – steamed rice."

Many people from the countryside in Laos did not even eat steamed rice until they went to Thailand as refugees. Even now some Laotian people feel that steamed rice is too light and that a real Lao meal demands sticky rice.

Sticky rice is normally eaten with the fingers. Reach into the serving basket. Using the index finger, middle finger and thumb pinch off the desired amount of sticky rice; a walnut–sized piece is fine. Work it between the thumb and two fingers forming a shallow depression in the lump of rice. This is then used to scoop out a tidbit of food or can be dipped into the sauce. Being careful not to drip the chili sauce on your clothes, pop it into your mouth Lao–style. Below are instructions for making Lao sticky rice. Once you acquire a taste for it you will crave it, so be careful.

Ingredients

4 cups of sticky rice
1 1/2 gallon water
large bowl
Aluminum steamer pot for sticky rice
Bamboo steamer tray with cover
Sticky rice bamboo serving basket

Preparation

In the large bowl soak 4 cups of sticky rice in 1 gallon of water for 2 hours. Drain the sticky rice into the bamboo steamer tray. Add 1/2 gallon of water to aluminum steamer pot and bring to a boil. Place the bamboo steamer tray with the sticky rice on top of the pot of boiling water. Cover and steam for 45 minutes. When rice is cooked pack the sticky rice into bamboo serving baskets which will keep the sticky rice warm and soft for a long time.

To my many loyal patrons I finally give you the book that so many of you have been requesting for so long.

Daovone Xayavong
Dara Restaurant
Berkeley, California
March, 2000

FOREWORD

As is appropriate in a foreword such as this, I begin by expressing a warm welcome to *Taste of Laos* and its author Daovone Xayavong, all the warmer because it will take its place on a shelf which is sparsely populated. Remarkably little has been written, in any language, about the food and cookery of Laos (the country) or Lao (the most numerous of the many ethnic groups therein).

Among the countries of Southeast Asia, Laos is the most mysterious and the least fully explored. In beauty and charm it is unsurpassed but in terms of population and power it counts for little among big neighbors such as China, Vietnam and Thailand. However, despite being relatively small and landlocked it has maintained with remarkable success its own culture, in the kitchen as well as in architecture, folklore and other aspects.

French control of Laos, which lasted from 1893 to the end of the 1940s, left its mark in many ways, but not much in the field of food and cookery. The relatively numerous Lao whose higher education took place in France acquired a taste for French bread and croissants and French wines, of which the bread at least remained available (and excellent) in the capital for the rest of the 20th century. But the Lao went right on cooking their own foods in their own ways, and even in the capital of Vientiane, French restaurant culture never had more than a tiny toehold, which depended on the continuing presence of French people.

However, this is not the first time I have written an introduction to a book of Lao recipes. I had the honour of doing just that back in the 1970s, when I became publisher and part–editor of the recipe notebooks of Phia Sing, the former royal chef at the Palace in Luang Prabang. This was a very instructive experience for me. I thought that I knew a lot about the foodways of Laos, having lived and worked there for two years, and having published a book on the *Fish and Fish Dishes of Laos*,[1] which had involved a lot of activity in the fish markets and also in Lao kitchens. However, the need to explain all about the ingredients and techniques in Phia Sing's recipes made me realise how much more I had to learn, and did learn before the resulting book, *Traditional Recipes of Laos*,[2] could be published.

I mention Phia Sing's recipes partly because his collection was and remains, to the best of my knowledge, unique in Southeast Asia as a meticulous record of an indigenous cuisine. Moreover, the record was created by someone who was and remains unique among writers on Asian foods. I have compared Phia Sing, in respect of his many accomplishments, to Leonardo da Vinci, and there are good grounds for this comparison. Phia Sing was not only the royal chef. He was also Royal Master of Ceremonies, at a court of many and beautiful ceremonies, physician, architect, choreographer, sculptor, painter, and poet, besides being tutor of the Royal Princes. Truly an extraordinary man.

Another reason for citing his recipes is that chance (as I see it) or the activities of be-nevolent spirits (as many Lao would think) played a decisive part in ensuring their survival. Had not the then Crown Prince paused on his own doorstep, while bidding me farewell after an interview, and asked me to wait a moment while he looked in an upstairs storeroom for 'something which might interest you', and had he not been able to locate the recipe notebooks where they lay, put aside in a place known to no one else and almost forgotten by himself, the two notebooks containing the manu-script recipes might well have been lost to sight forever. As it was, I had the loan of them, was able to make photocopies, and could subsequently, with my daughter, Jen-nifer, organise a team of Lao friends to transcribe them from the antique palace script which Phia Sing had used into modern Lao and translate them into English. The reac-tions of these Lao friends to my tale of the miraculous 'discovery' of the recipe books were illuminating. Of course, they said, the Crown Prince would have remembered at just the right moment – the spirits would have seen to that.

The relaxed attitude, which is natural to those who believe that spirits will benevo-lently intervene in human affairs when necessary, applies also to culinary matters. Jen-nifer and I would agonise over some 'difficult' ingredients such as dried palate of a water buffalo, which occurs fairly often. But then one of the Lao would explain that this need not be a problem for cooks outside Laos, with easier access to seafood. The dried palates were actually a substitute for prawns, which the Lao would prefer if they could obtain them! I still wonder a little about this, but I do not doubt the validity of the lesson it taught me: not to be too preoccupied, when working on Lao dishes, with de-tails which would not worry the Lao themselves.

This point is highly relevant to the *Taste of Laos* which will be in regular use by many people who are not merely outside Laos but thousands of miles away. Such people may well be aware of Thai cuisine, in the form in which it has spread around the world in the last quarter of the twentith century, and may wonder how far Lao cuisine differs from it.

Well, I had occasion to think about this question myself recently. I know that some would dismiss it as simplistic, given the marked regional variations in Thai foodways (which make for a group of cuisines rather than a single one), and allowing for the fact that the north of Thailand contains more ethnic Lao than Laos itself. Yet it is a pertinent question, and consideration of it helps to highlight the particular characteristics of the Lao diet and ways of cooking. To be sure, there are no dramatic differences. But to eat for a few days in Bangkok and then to have the next few days in Vientiane (or Luang Prabang, the former royal capital) would convince anyone that the differences are there. Some of these differences are of emphasis rather than substance. The Lao use much more mint than the Thai, while going along with the Thai in frequent use of cori-ander and basil. They also use more garlic and fresh ginger; the Lao name for ginger is *khing* and in the currency of the spirit world, in which many Lao believe, it is gold.

Also, for obvious reasons, the Lao eat a higher proportion of freshwater fish than the Thai people (although in areas far from the sea this generalization may not hold). And they have more dishes based on these fish. Their *padek*, a variant of the ubiquitous Southeast Asian fish sauces (*nam pla* in Thailand, *nuoc mam* in Vietnam) is a rough prod-uct containing bits of fish and rice husks; it has a powerful smell, so the large earthen-ware pot containing it is usually stored outside the house. It is specific to Laos and the Lao-inhabited territories of northern Thailand, and its frequent use as an ingredient in

Lao dishes helps to make them distinctive.

What is certainly true is that the Lao people are notably discriminating in their choice of ingredients (no inferior produce finds its way into their markets); in their choice of cooking techniques for particular ingredients or dishes (for example, they have numerous words meaning 'to fry', not just one); and in their tastes. On this last point, it is pertinent to note that Phia Sing uses two different words for 'taste', *jae* and *sim*. The former is appropriate when tasting uncooked mixtures. It means to touch the ingredients with your fingertip and then put the fingertip to your lips, thus tasting only a very small amount. The latter is normally used for tasting cooked ingredients, when it would be usual to take a tiny spoonful.

Turning to the conclusion of a meal, so often attended in the western world by mountains of debris and stacks of dishes and cutlery to be 'washed up'[3], one may find in Laos that there is nothing left except an empty sticky rice basket. As I wrote elsewhere, referring to the common Lao practice of eating with the fingers: "this can be done delicately by wrapping up mouthfuls of food in edible leaves. *Phan* is a verb which indicates the use of such leaves to wrap up morsels of food, or a mixture of morsels, before eating them. The Lao often have one platter of edible leaves, another or others of meat or fish or vegetables, and a bowl of sauce for dunking. The leaves enable them to eat the food, with the sauce, without employing any cutlery.

However, let no one be misled by this last passage into thinking that, in order to be authentic in eating Lao dishes, one must use one's fingers. The concept of 'authenticity' is foreign to Lao minds. One is expected to adapt their foodways to suit oneself – and what could be better than that. On that note I repeat my warm welcome to the *Taste of Laos* and wish this valuable new book and those who use it every success and much pleasure.

Alan Davidson
Chelsea, London
February, 2000

Alan Davidson was born in 1924 in Northern Ireland. His initial career, in the British Navy in and after the Second World War, took him for the first time to Southeast Asia. His next career in the British Diplomatic Service took him back there as British Ambassador to Laos from 1973 to 1975. Since then he has spent over 20 years writing *The Oxford Companion to Food*. Living in Chelsea, London, with his American wife, Jane, he is now working on studies of the Hollywood screwball comedy heroines of the 1930s and early 1940s.

[1] Alan Davidson, *Fish and Fish Dishes of Laos*, with illustrations by Soun Vannithone and other Lao artists, Imprimerie Nationale, Vientiane, 1974; then in a second revised impression for Charles E. Tuttle, Rutland, Vermont and Tokyo, 1975; and now being republished by Prospect Books, Totnes, Devon in 2000

[2] Phia Sing, *Traditional Recipes of Laos* (translated by Phouangphet Vannithone and Boon Song Klausner, edited by Alan and Jennifer Davidson), with illustrations by Soun Vannithone, Prospect Books, London, 1981.

[3] I think my book *The Oxford Companion to Food*, Oxford University Press, London and New York, 1999, is probably the first encyclopaedic food book to include an essay on washing up, and I enjoyed writing this. I omitted, however, to mention that in some cultures there may be nothing to wash up.

Introduction

OK, the first thing to say is that you don't have to do the thing with the ant eggs.

There are two main reasons why I (and, more than likely, you) acquire "exotic"[1] cookbooks:
1. To learn about another culture through knowledge of their quaint and amusing (in other words, very different from mine) ways of dealing with food; and
2. To get some wonderful new and usual recipes that can be made with ingredients you'll find right there in Santa Barbara or Cleveland or wherever you live, and which you can serve to your family or your bridge club, or bring to the pot luck without fear of someone dialing 911 for the food police.

In the best of such books, and this is indeed one of those, both of the above issues are addressed. In other words, at the same time that you are learning about the legendary northern Lao Ant Egg Soup, you also have the opportunity to create, in your very own kitchen, a wide array of dishes that will be as popular on your table as they are in the fishing villages along the Mekong River. Jumping Shrimp Salad. Crispy Lemon Grass Chicken. Catfish Salad.

Speaking of Catfish Salad, it is time for a diversion to reflect on traffic patterns in downtown Berkeley, California. In a three-block area, along Shattuck Avenue, is a district known as the "Gourmet Ghetto," where Chez Panisse opened a few decades ago, and many other restaurants, the good, the bad, and the ugly, followed. On one particular corner (the northeast corner of Shattuck and Cedar), so many restaurants came and went, sometimes in a matter of weeks from grand opening to ignominious closing, that locals began speculating whether that spot had bad juju or inauspicious *feng shui* or a gypsy curse or something.

Then one day, a few years ago, a friend said, "Come with me. I have discovered something truly wonderful": Dara, a Laotian restaurant, at the infamous corner of Shattuck and Cedar, where the catfish salad is something to write home about, whether your home is on the Mekong or on Main Street. We went. And after experiencing the catfish salad (after the Laotian-style hot and sour soup, and before the Vientiane Mango Fool), it was abundantly clear to me that there was no curse on this corner; there just had not been a restaurant of the quality of Dara there, to justify its existence at the gateway to the Ghetto.

I've been back to Dara many times over the past six or seven years: always positive[2], always interesting. And so I was very pleased, indeed, when founder/chef Daovone Xayavong decided to share some of her best and most popular recipes.

It is said that Laotian food is the last "undiscovered" cuisine of South East Asia. China. Taiwan. Korea. Vietnam. Thailand. Burma. Cambodia. Those foods all have a lot to recommend then. And now comes Laos, and some would say that whoever organizes such things has saved the best for last.

One thing I like so much about these dishes and these recipes is that many of them (OK, not the ant eggs) take things you already know about, and deal with them not just in unexpected combinations (papaya and garlic, peanuts and cabbage, crab meat and ginger), but in unusual (to the western kitchen) yet very doable cooking methods. One example: taking cooked sticky rice, roasting it until it is crisp, and grinding it into powder, which becomes an ingredient for a wide range of soups, salads, and entrees.

Another thing I really like about this book is that the author enhances her recipes with vignettes about the food and culture of Laos and very helpful explanations of the ingredients and the cooking techniques. The story of fiddlehead fern-gathering parties, for instance, as a preface to the Fiddlehead Fern Soup recipe.

Finally, some thoughts on sparkling arpeggios. I do admire the art of restaurant reviewing, since it requires not only a deep understanding of food and cooking, but a command of a specialized sort of language I've never been able to achieve. Perhaps there is some secret correspondence course one can take, or maybe one is just born with those skills.

So, in this frame of mind, I have been gazing at one of the splendid reviews that the Dara Lao has received, thinking that reviewer Joan Zoloth, of the Oakland Tribune said just what I would have said about the marvelous Nam Lao dish, if only it had occurred to me to come up with those arpeggios, and a cornucopia to boot. The heck with it. I shall quote her instead:

> "What is most striking about [Dara Lao] cuisine is that the tastes present sparkling arpeggios within each dish. The Nam Lao, for example, is a cornucopia of different ingredients served on a plate-crunchy bean sprouts, fresh cilantro, thin rice noodles, and a bowl of chicken that has been marinated with herbs, and then sautéed and mixed with chili. We rolled the ingredients into translucent rice wrappers. It was a fresh and exciting combination that awoke the senses."

And I bring you the wonderful news that you do not need to journey either to Laos or to the corner of Shattuck and Cedar in Berkeley for this experience. With the assistance of the Nam Lao recipe right there in the Appetizer section, and almost 100 other recipes that don't involve ant eggs, plus two that do, those arpeggios can sparkle right in your own dining room.

John Bear
March 26, 2000
Berkeley, California

---

[1] Exotic," that is, to people in North America, in just the way *Joy of Cooking* would be considered "exotic" in Laos. T-bone steak, baked potato, and raddichio salad indeed."

[2] Well, almost always. There was once a strange green soup that others really liked, but it just wasn't my cup of, well, green soup. And I have not tried the ant eggs. Probably never will. Such is life.

FRESH SPINACH WARPS

APPETIZERS

DEEP FRIED QUAIL
EGG ROLLS
BAG OF GOLD
CRISPY SEA PERCH with MANGO CHILI DIP
FRESH SPINACH WRAPS
CRAB CAKES
DEEP FRIED MUSHROOMS
SEAFOOD KABOBS
HEAVENLY BEEF
FRESH ROLLS
STICKY RICE KABOB
SATAY
SOUR PORK IN BANANA LEAF
HOT AND SWEET GREEN MANGO
MUSHROOM CHILI DIP
SPICY ANCHOVY DIP
MEKONG CATFISH CHILI DIP
ANT EGG OMELETTE

NOOK TOD
DEEP FRIED QUAIL

Fried quail is wonderful finger food. It is one of the most popular appetizers served in Dara Restaurant. It is easy to make, easy to serve and very easy to enjoy. Chewing on the bones is quite acceptable behavior.

Ingredients

4 quail, cleaned and cut into halves
8 cloves garlic, crushed
1 stalk lemon grass, minced
1 tablespoon oyster sauce
1 tablespoon soy sauce
1 tablespoon fish sauce
1 teaspoon sugar
1/2 teaspoon black pepper
1/2 teaspoon coriander seed powder
2 tablespoons cooking wine
Oil for frying

Preparation

Prepare marinade by mixing together the garlic, lemon grass, oyster sauce, soy sauce, fish sauce, sugar, black pepper, coriander seed powder, and wine. Marinate the quail in the mixture and refrigerate for at least 6 hours; overnight is fine.

Heat oil in a wok. Deep-fry the quail until golden brown and crispy. Remove from the oil and drain. Arrange on a small serving platter atop lettuce leaves and shredded carrots.

Serve with Deep Fried Quail Dipping Sauce listed in the Dipping Sauce section.

Serves 4

KA YO TOD
EGG ROLLS

Egg rolls are without a doubt the best known and most popular Asian appetizer to emigrate to the West. Local versions are also served in China, Vietnam, Thailand, Indonesia, and the Philippines. One of the secrets for a crispy egg roll is to start with a thin wrapper. It is no longer necessary to make these by hand. Very good commercially made wrappers are available in most markets. Unused wrappers freeze very well. Just make sure you wrap them well before freezing.

Ingredients

12 spring roll wrappers
1/4 pound ground pork
5 dried Chinese black mushrooms, soak in water until soft and dice
1/2 tablespoon soy sauce
1/2 teaspoon salt
1 teaspoon sugar
1/2 teaspoon black pepper
1 cup mung bean sprouts, roots removed
1 cup julienned cabbage
1 cup julienned carrots
3 oz clear noodles, soak in water until soft and cut into 1" length
Oil for frying
Sealing paste*

Preparation

Heat 1/2 tablespoon of the oil in a wok. Stir-fry ground pork until cooked. Add dried mushrooms, soy sauce, salt, sugar, black pepper, bean sprouts, cabbage, carrots, and noodles. Stir briefly; remove from wok and cool. Place 1 tablespoon of the filling along the edge of the wrap and fold the wrap over the filling. Fold both ends over to enclose filling, roll up tightly and seal with the sealing paste.

In a wok heat oil to 375º F. Deep-fry 4–6 rolls at a time until crispy and golden brown. Remove and drain. Serve with Egg Roll Dipping Sauce list in the Dipping Sauce section.

Serves 4

* Mix 1 tablespoon flour with 2 tablespoon water stirring over low heat until thoroughly mixed.

THONG THONG
BAG OF GOLD

Reward your guests with a good luck "bag of gold" as an appetizer. They are fun to make, look picturesque on the serving platter and are much cheaper than the real thing.

Ingredients

10 egg roll wraps cut into 4 pieces each
1/2 pound ground pork
2 garlic cloves, minced
5 cilantro stalks (or 1 plant with root), chopped
1/2 pound shrimp shelled, deveined and chopped
4 dried Chinese black mushrooms, soak in water until soft and dice
1/4 pound clear noodles, soak in water until soft, drain and chop
A pinch of black pepper
1/2 teaspoon salt
1 teaspoon fish sauce
1 teaspoon sugar
4 green onions, green tops only, for tying bags
4 cups oil for frying

Preparation

Heat 1 tablespoon of the oil in a wok. When oil is hot add garlic, cilantro, ground pork, shrimp, dried mushrooms, clear noodles, black pepper, salt, fish sauce and sugar. Stir-fry the mixture until cooked. Remove from wok to cool. Put a piece of wrap on a plate. Place a teaspoon of the stir-fried mixture in the middle of the wrap. Bring the 4 corners of the filled wrap packet together and twist to close like a bag. Tie each bag with a green onion top. Heat the oil in a wok over high heat, when oil is hot carefully add 5 or 6 of the bags and deep-fry until golden brown. Remove from wok and drain. Serve with Bag of Gold Hot Sauce listed in the Dipping Sauce section.

Serves 4

PA TOD MAMUANG NAMAPLA
CRISPY SEA PERCH with MANGO CHILI DIP

Pa is fish in Lao. Many varieties of fish abound in Laos. Very few are available outside of Southeast Asia. I have tried to substitute readily available fish for the ones I would use in my home country. I, as many Lao, love catfish, of which we have more than a few kinds. There is even a vegetarian catfish, pa beuk, although close to extinction it is considered by many to be the king of Laotian fish. For more information on fish in Laos I recommend reading Alan Davidson, who books are listed at the end of his foreword.

Ingredients

1 pound sea perch fillets, sliced into one inch squares
1 cup all purpose flour
1/2 teaspoon salt
4 cups oil
Assortment of sliced vegetables, such as cucumber, eggplant, etc.

Preparation

Combine flour and salt in a large bowl and mix well. Coat the sea perch and set aside. Meanwhile heat oil in a wok over a high heat. When the oil is hot, deep-fry the sea perch until golden brown. Remove from the wok and drain.

Arrange the sea perch and vegetables on a platter and serve with the Mango Chili Dip listed in the Dipping Sauce section.

Serves 4

MIANG KAM
FRESH SPINACH WRAPS

A typical Lao way to serve food is to present an array of various ingredients on a serving platter with something in which to wrap them all up. The wrappers can be rice paper or as in this recipe a leafy vegetable. What we have is a communal snack where each person selects the favored ingredients, adds sauce, rolls his or her own delicacy and pops it deftly and cleanly into their mouth.

This recipe originated with the Lao royal family who entertains a lot. Miang Kam is served as a snack to Lao subjects who come to the royal palace.

Ingredients

12 large spinach leaves; (trimmed lettuce leaves can be substituted)
1 tablespoon shredded coconut, toasted
1 tablespoon chopped, roasted peanuts
1 tablespoon chopped dried shrimp
1 stalk lemon grass, chopped
1 tablespoon finely slivered fresh ginger
1 shallot, thinly sliced
8 thin slices of lemon
2 tablespoon ground crispy sticky rice

Preparation

In a mixing bowl, gently toss together the coconut, peanuts, dried shrimp, lemon grass, ginger and shallot together. Set aside. You can also put each of these ingredients in individual serving bowls and arrange them on the serving platter with the other elements of miang kam.

Arrange the spinach leaves on a large serving platter along with the bowl of sauce and the bowl of miang kam mixture. Put lemon slices and crispy rice in small serving bowls and place on the serving platter.

To eat, sprinkle each leaf with a small amount of the mixture, add a slice of lemon, a bit of the crispy rice and 1/2 teaspoon of the sauce. Roll up and eat. Look in the Sauce Section to find the recipe for Fresh Spinach Wrap Sauce listed in the Dipping Sauce section.

Serves 4

POO JA
CRAB CAKES

Even though this recipe has been around since the days of French colonialism in Indo-China, it is surprisingly up-to-date. If you like your crab cakes to have a little more punch, this is the recipe for you.

Ingredients

1/2 pound cooked crab meat
4 eggs, beaten
1 cup breadcrumbs
1 stalk celery, chopped
1 teaspoon salt
2 kaffir lime leaves, thinly sliced
1 tablespoon red curry paste
1 teaspoon sugar
3 cups oil

Garnish with sliced cucumber and carrots, and shredded lettuce

Preparation

In medium mixing bowl, combine eggs, 1/2 cup of the breadcrumbs, chopped celery, salt, red curry paste, kaffir lime leaves and sugar. Fold in the crabmeat. Shape into 8 cakes and coat with the remaining breadcrumbs. In a large skillet heat the oil and deep-fry the crab cakes until golden brown on both sides. Drain on paper towel and serve with Sweet and Sour Sauce listed in the Dipping Sauce section.

Serves 4

TOD HED
DEEP FRIED MUSHROOMS

In Laos I would use the hed khao or hed bod mushroom for this dish. Hed is Lao for mushroom. You may use whatever mushrooms you like. Sliced portobello mushrooms are also very good for this dish.

Ingredients

1/2 pound fresh white mushrooms
1 cup all purpose flour
1/3 cup water
1 teaspoon cornstarch
1/2 teaspoon salt
A pinch of black pepper
1 egg
4 cups oil

Preparation

Clean the mushrooms. Blanch briefly in boiling water. Remove from water, pat dry with a paper towel and set aside.

In a mixing bowl combine flour, water, cornstarch, salt, black pepper, and egg together. Beat until smooth enough to use as a batter.

Heat the oil in a frying pan to about 330 F. Dip the mushrooms into the batter and deep fry until golden brown. Remove from the oil and drain well.

Serve with sauce of your choice. Look in the Dipping Sauce section for a selection. I prefer a hot sauce or jéo som with this appetizer.

Serves 4

SATAY TALAY
SEAFOOD KABOBS

Grilled fresh seafood is ubiquitous in the street markets and at the fairs in Laos. Served with rice and larger portions this delicious appetizer makes a wonderful main course as well.

Ingredients

6 Fresh mushrooms cut in half
2 dozen large scallops
1 dozen large shrimp, shelled and deveined
6 small squid, cleaned and cut into 3 pieces each
2 each green and red bell peppers cut into 2-inch squares
1 tablespoon oil
1 teaspoon sugar
1 tablespoon fish sauce
1 tablespoon soy sauce
2 garlic cloves, minced
1/2 teaspoon black pepper
1 teaspoon Chinese cooking wine
6 bamboo skewers

Preparation

In a large bowl combine oil, sugar, fish sauce, soy sauce, garlic, black pepper and wine. Gently toss in the mushrooms, scallops, shrimp, squid, and bell peppers. Alternate the seafood with the vegetables on the skewers, saving the marinade for basting.

Lightly oil the heated grill. Grill each skewer for 6 to 8 minutes turning each kabob carefully at least twice. Brush with marinade after turning.

Serve on a platter with cucumber and peanut salad. See recipe in sauce section.

Serves 6

SINE SAVANH
HEAVENLY BEEF

In Laos where the days are long and the sun is hot we dry the beef outside. In more temperate climates or on an overcast day you will have to dry the beef in the oven. Don't forget to marinate the beef first. Heavenly Beef is very popular not only for snacks but also for breakfast. It goes well with sticky rice. We refer to this combination as the "beef couple."

Ingredients

1 pound beef flank steak, cut into thin strips and sun dried*
10 garlic cloves, minced
2 tablespoons cooking wine
1 tablespoon soy sauce
1 teaspoon salt
1 tablespoon sugar
1 teaspoon black pepper
2 tablespoons sesame seeds
4 cups cooking oil

Preparation

In a large bowl mix the garlic, wine, soy sauce, salt, sugar, black pepper, and sesame seeds. Mix thoroughly. Add the flank strips, mix well and marinate for at least two hours. Remove from the marinade and dry.

Heat oil in a wok over medium heat. When oil is hot Deep–fry the dried beef until crispy. Drain and serve.

*Arrange the strips of marinated flank steak on a bamboo tray and dry in the hot sun for a full day. Alternatively you can place the beef in the oven on the lowest possible setting for a few hours. You want the beef to be dried (think beef jerky) but not so dry that it crumbles. Check on it occasionally to prevent over drying

Serves 4

NAM LAO
FRESH ROLLS

"Nam Lao is a cornucopia of different ingredients served on a plate with crunchy bean sprouts, fresh cilantro, thin rice noodles and a bowl of chicken that has been marinated with herbs, and then sautéed and mixed with chili. We rolled the ingredients into translucent rice wrappers. It was a fresh and exciting combination that awoke the senses." — from a review of Dara Restaurant by Joan Zoloth in the Oakland Tribune.

Ingredients

12 rice paper wraps
1/2 pound diced chicken breast or beef flank steak
2 tablespoons oil
1/2 teaspoon salt
1 cup chicken stock
1 cup bean sprouts
1 cup shredded lettuce
1/4 cup of water
2 green onions cut into 1-inch lengths
1 cucumber, thinly sliced
1 bunch cilantro, chopped
1 cup Rice noodles, cooked and slightly chopped

Preparation

First prepare the Tamarind Sauce. Look in Dipping Sauce section for the recipe.

In the same pan in which you made the Tamarind Sauce briefly sauté the chicken or beef with one tablespoon of oil and 1/2 teaspoon of salt. Add chicken stock and cook over medium heat until meat is done. Remove to a small bowl.

Technique for preparing and wrapping Nam Lao

Soak each sheet of rice paper in a flat, shallow bowl of warm water for about 15 seconds. Pick up the wrap with the fingertips of both hands and let the water drip off before placing the rice paper sheet on a flat surface. Arrange a little each of the lettuce, green onions, cilantro, cucumber slices, rice noodles, chicken and tamarind sauce near the edge of rice paper. Fold rice paper over the filling. Continue to roll and seal. Wrapping your own nam lao makes for fun eating and is good for having long conversations.

Serves 4

KAO JEE PING
STICKY RICE KABOB

Next time you grill seafood kabobs why not toss in a few skewers of sticky rice kabobs then it would be a real Lao barbecue.

Ingredients

2 Eggs, beaten
A pinch of salt
2 tablespoon Salad oil
2 cups steamed sticky rice*
Bamboo skewers, soaked in water

Preparation

Combine steamed sticky rice with salt. Knead thoroughly. Divide into 8 pieces. Mold each portion into an oval shape and thread it onto the bamboo skewer. Coat the rice kabobs with the beaten egg. Lightly coat the hot grill with oil and grill the kabobs for 2 minutes. Brush the top of the kabobs lightly with oil, rotate and grill for an additional 2 minutes.

Arrange on a platter with lettuce leaves. Serve with peanut sauce.

*Soak sticky rice in water for 2 hours and steam in a steamer for 45 minutes.

Serves 4

SIN SEAP
SATAY

Satay is another all-time favorite Asian appetizer to emigrate to the West. Two of the secrets for crowd-pleasing satay are a tangy marinade and a tasty dipping sauce. Of course good quality meat is always a good starting point for succulent satay.

Ingredients

2 pounds Chicken or beef, cut into 3/4 inch cubes
4 tablespoon oil
Skewers for grilling

Spice Paste Marinade Ingredients

1 tablespoon soy sauce
8 shallots, sliced
8 garlic cloves, sliced
2 slices fresh galangal root (or 1 tablespoon galangal powder)
2 slices of fresh ginger
4 fresh chilies, seeded and sliced
1 tablespoon black pepper
1 tablespoon powered coriander
1 tablespoon fish sauce
2 tablespoons Palm sugar, brown sugar can also be used

Preparation for Spice Paste Marinade

Combine all paste ingredients in a food processor. Push pulse a few times until the ingredients turn into a paste. In a pan over medium heat sauté the paste briefly in hot oil. Cool the spice mixture and rub over the meat cubes. Cover and let marinate in the refrigerator for one to two hours.

Spear the cubes of meat on the skewers. Turning frequently, grill over high heat until cooked.

Serve with peanut sauce and cucumber relish. See Dipping Sauce section for recipes.

Serves 4

SOM MOO
SOUR PORK IN BANANA LEAF

This is a very typical and popular dish in Laos. If the idea of eating uncooked pork makes you squeamish you might want to pass on this one. Kneading it with the other ingredients cures the pork.

Ingredients

8 fresh chilies
1 Slices fresh ginger
1/4 pound Lean pork, ground
1 cup steamed pork skin, finely diced
2 tablespoons salt
3 tablespoons minced garlic

1 Banana leaf cut into six-inch squares
String or rubber band to secure pork bundle

Garnish: lettuce leaves, sliced fresh ginger and chilies

Preparation

Combine all ingredients in a large bowl. Knead until mixture forms a sticky batter. Place the mixture in the center of the banana leaf. Fold over the ends to form a secure envelope. Tighten with string or rubber bands and store in cool part of the kitchen, but not in the refrigerator otherwise the pork will not cure. Check in 2 to 3 days. If the bundle has become sour it is ready. Remove the banana leaf, slice and arrange on a platter on a bed of lettuce. Top with slices of fresh ginger and chilies.

Serves 4

MAMUANG NAMPLA WAN
HOT AND SWEET GREEN MANGO

Asians in general and Lao in particular love green fruit, especially green mangoes. If you find this traditional appetizer appeals to your palate, then you are an honorary Lao.

Ingredients

1/4 cup water
3 tablespoons fish sauce
1/2 teaspoon soy sauce
1/2 cup Palm sugar
10 shallots, finely sliced
4 fresh chilies, seeded and chopped
1/4 cup dried shrimp, ground
4 young green mangoes, sliced and soaked in water for 5 minutes

Preparation for the dipping sauce

Heat the water in a pot. Add fish sauce, soy sauce, and palm sugar. Mix well and boil until mixture thickens. Set aside to cool. After mixture has cooled add shallots and fresh chilies and dried shrimp. Pour into a small serving bowl.

Place the bowl of dipping sauce in the center of a serving platter and arrange the mango slices around the bowl. Dip the mango slices into the sauce.

Serves 4

JEL HED POUK
MUSHROOM CHILI DIP

There are dozens of edible varieties of mushrooms in Laos. Hed means mushroom while pouak means termite. The "termite mushroom" grows in damp places on dead and decaying trees. For this recipe oyster mushrooms make a good substitute for the hed pouak mushroom.

With this dish you serve a variety of fresh vegetables such as cucumber, lettuce, eggplant, celery carrots; you name it, for dipping. Mushroom Chili Dip is also excellent with sticky rice. It is especially good for people on a diet as it goes well with almost all fresh vegetables.

Ma keua phoung a small Asian eggplant that grows in clusters and looks like large peas is traditionally eaten with this dip. See glossary under eggplant for details.

Ingredients

1/2 pound oyster mushrooms
3–5 fresh red chilies, seeded
4 shallots, peeled
1 green onion
2 cloves garlic, peeled
1/2 teaspoon salt
1 tablespoon fish sauce
1 tablespoon cilantro chopped

Various vegetables for dipping such as
cucumbers, lettuce, eggplant, celery, carrots

Preparation

Roast the mushrooms, shallots, green onion, garlic and chilies over an open fire until slightly charred. Transfer to a mortar and pound with a pestle until a paste is formed. Alternately, process in a food processor until smooth. Add salt, fish sauce, and cilantro. Mix well and pour into a serving bowl.

Serve with sticky rice and your choice of vegetables.

Serves 4

JEL PLA DAEK
SPICY ANCHOVY DIP

During the war the people in the city had to teach new refugees from the country-side about pla daek (Anchovies). Because of the strong smell they were reluctant to try it. But it soon became one of the foods that helped their generation to survive living in suburbs while they worked the fields outside the urban area.

Ingredients

1/2 cup of anchovy fillets, chopped
5 fresh chilies, seeded and sliced
1 stalk lemon grass, finely chopped
4 cloves garlic, minced
2 slices fresh galanga, chopped

Fresh vegetables of your choice for dipping;
Ong choi, ma kheur pro (small Thai eggplant), cucumber, carrots Chinese long beans, zucchini, turnip, squash, wax gourd.

Preparation

Pound chilies, lemon grass, garlic, and galanga in a motar with a pestle to a fine paste, adding a bit of water if necessary. Add anchovies and mix thoroughly. Scrape into a small bowl and serve with your choice of fresh or steamed vegetables.

Serves 4

CHEO PLA DUK
MEKONG CATFISH CHILI DIP

As you have discovered if you have seen some of the other recipes in my cookbook Lao people love to dip vegetables into a variety of hot and spicy dips. This is one of my favorites and it also goes well with both sticky rice and crispy rice cakes.

Since Mekong catfish is not readily available outside of Southeast Asia you should use whatever catfish is available in your area.

Ingredients

1/2 pound Mekong catfish fillet, grilled and chopped
10 chilies, roasted
2 shallots, roasted
4 cloves garlic, roasted
1/2 tablespoon shrimp paste
4 Lao eggplant (ma kheua pro), grilled
or 1 Chinese eggplant, grilled
2 cups soup stock
1 tablespoon fish sauce
1 tablespoon lemon juice
1 tablespoon palm sugar
variety of fresh, cut vegetables to dip

Preparation

Pound chilies, shallots, garlic, and shrimp paste together well in a mortar and pestle. Add grilled catfish fillets and eggplants. Continue pounding until all ingredients are well combined. Add soup stock, fish sauce, lemon juice, and palm sugar. Mix well. Pour the sauce into a dipping bowl and place in the center of a serving platter. Surround the bowl with various vegetables to be dipped.

Serves 4

KOA KHAI MOOD
ANT EGG OMELETTE

Ant eggs are available in may Thai and Vietnamese markets. For more on ant eggs see my recipe for Ant Egg Soup in the soup section.

Ingredients

3 eggs
1 cup ant eggs
4 cloves garlic, chopped
1/2 teaspoon black pepper
1/2 cup yellow onion, chopped
1 teaspoon fish sauce
2 tablespoons cilantro, chopped
2 tablespoon oil

Preparation

In a mixing bowl beat the eggs well and add all ingredients except the oil. Heat the oil in a frying pan or a wok over high. Add the egg mixture and cook until golden brown. Serve with rice and sweet and sour sauce.

Serves 2

TOFU COCONUT SOUP

SOUPS

VEGETARIAN STOCK
CHICKEN STOCK
BEEF STOCK
FIDDLEHEAD FERN SOUP
YOUNG BANANA TREE SOUP
ANT EGG SOUP
TOFU COCONUT MILK SOUP
HOT and SOUR CHICKEN SOUP
PRAWN COCONUT MILK SOUP
LAO BEEF SOUP

NAM TOM JAY
VEGETARIAN STOCK

This is a light and mild tasting vegetarian soup stock. To add a little more pizzazz to your steamed rice use soup stock instead of water.

Ingredients

1 1/2 pounds soybean sprouts
1 bunch of Chinese celery, chopped or
3 stalks American celery with leaves, sliced
2 onions, sliced
4 carrots, sliced
1/2 bunch of cilantro, chopped
1/4 teaspoon salt
8 cups water

Preparation

Place all vegetables in a large soup pot with water. Bring slowly to a boil. Reduce heat and simmer gently for about 30 minutes. Skim off any scum that first rises to the surface. Add salt, strain and cool.

NAM TOM GAI
CHICKEN STOCK

Good chicken stock is invaluable in any kitchen, even a Lao one. Almost any recipe that calls for water would be emboldened by using chicken stock instead. If you use chicken stock instead of water next time you make rice your guests will be impressed with how good your rice tastes.

Ingredients

2 pounds chicken backs, wings, necks, and bones
10 cups water
1 Chinese radish, chopped
1 bunch of Chinese celery chopped or
3 stalks of American celery, chopped
2 garlic cloves, peeled
5 bay leaves
Salt

Preparation

Wash chicken parts and place them in a stockpot. Add cold water and remaining ingredients except salt. Bring to a boil. Reduce heat, and simmer, skimming off the scum during the first 25 minutes of cooking. Partially cover stockpot and simmer for 2 hours. Salt to taste. Remove all the ingredients and strain the stock. Cool and re-frigerate stock. Remove the layer of fat from the top of the cooled stock before using.

NAM TOM KADUK
BEEF STOCK

Beef stock, better known as beef tea in some parts of Asia, makes an invigorating afternoon beverage.

Ingredients

5 pounds beef bones, cut into small pieces
6 quarts water
1 yellow onion, chopped
2 cilantro roots, chopped
A pinch of salt

Preparation

Wash beef bones and place them in a stockpot. Add water and remaining ingredients except salt. Bring to a boil. Reduce heat, and simmer, skimming off the scum during the first 25 minutes of cooking. Partially cover stockpot and simmer for 3 to 4 hours. Salt to taste. Remove all the ingredients and strain the stock. Cool and refrigerate stock. Remove the layer of fat from the top of the cooled stock.

KEANG PAK KOUD
FIDDLEHEAD FERN SOUP

This soup is a favorite among the hill tribes of northern Laos. During the April to July rainy season fiddlehead ferns grow in abundance along the small rivers in Laos. It is a traditional treat when one visits with friends during the season. Visitors enjoy accompanying their hosts on fiddlehead fern gathering excursions to the riverbanks where this delectable vegetable thrives. Young country girls often go on fern gathering trips in the afternoon to snip enough fern fronds for the dinner soup.

If you want to boost the flavor of this soup try using chicken or vegetarian soup stock instead of water.

Ingredients

6 cups of water, or stock
1/2 teaspoon salt
1 stalk lemon grass cut in half and smashed
1 1/2 tablespoons fish sauce
1/2 pound dried sea perch
2 fresh chilies, broken in half
1/2 pound fiddle head fern fronds
1 green onion cut into 1" lengths

Preparation

In a soup pot bring water to a boil and add salt, lemon grass, fish sauce, dried sea perch, and chilies. Boil until sea perch is tender, about 30 minutes. Add fiddlehead ferns and green onions. Mix well, bring to a boil and serve.

Shopping Tip

Select small fiddlehead fern fronds (about 1 1/2 to 2 inches in diameter) with tightly rolled, bright green, firm coils. Avoid those with thick tails, a sign of toughness.

Serves 4

KANG YOUK
YOUNG BANANA TREE SOUP

Traditionally Lao people would go to the jungle or a banana farm for the banana tree. Now young banana trees are available in the market. If you can't find young banana tree in your local market, try making this soup with hearts of palm.

The northern Lao hill tribe people who live along the banks of the Nam Guam River have a real passion for this soup. On special feast days such as ghost worshipping and Basi New Year this dish is a must. Before the wedding the bride and groom enjoy meeting in the jungle to find a young banana tree for their banquet soup.

Ingredients

2 pounds pork ribs, cut into pieces
4 cups water or chicken stock
1 to 1 1/2 pounds of a young banana tree *
2 fresh chilies, broken in half
1 bunch young tamarind tips
Or 1/2 cup tamarind juice
1 green onion cut into 1" lengths
1 1/2 tablespoons fish sauce
Salt

Preparation

Place the pork ribs and water in a pot and bring to a boil. Skim the fat and other residue off the surface and reduce the heat. Continue boiling and skimming for 20 minutes. When the broth is clear add young banana tree pieces, young tamarind tips, fish sauce, fresh chilies and green onion. Bring back to boil and remove from heat, salt to taste, and serve.

* Take a section of a young, small banana tree. Remove the leaves and outer skin. Peel and slice the soft and tender parts into 1−inch squares, soak in water for 10 minutes and drain.

Serves 4

KEANG KHAI MOOD
ANT EGG SOUP

Ant egg soup is legendary in northern Laos and northeast Thailand. Once tasted, it is sure to become a favorite. The best eggs come from the ants that live on the mango and logan trees.

The tree ant builds large nests that hang under the branches of the tree. We gather the eggs, which are shaped like small peanuts by knocking the nest into a bucket of water held underneath the nest. The recently hatched ants float on the surface of the water. We scoop them off and discard them.

Ant eggs not only have a lot of protein but also have a lovely crunchy texture and a mildly sour taste. The unique sour taste of tamarind in this soup is also delightful.

In Laos we often use som poy – a sour leaf, available almost everywhere in Laos – instead of tamarind when making this soup at home.

Ingredients

3 cups chicken stock
1 stalk lemon grass, cut in half and smashed
1 teaspoon salt
1 1/2 tablespoons fish sauce
4 fresh chilies, broken in half
1 bunch young tamarind tips
Or 2 1/2 tablespoons tamarind juice
1 shallot, cut in half
2 cups ant eggs *
1 green onion, cut into 1" lengths

Preparation

In a pot bring chicken stock to a boil. Add lemon grass, salt, fish sauce, chilies, shallot and tamarind and boil for about 15 minutes. Add ant eggs and green onions. Remove from heat and serve.

* Although we use fresh ant eggs in Laos, outside of SE Asia you will have to settle for frozen ant eggs, which are available in most Vietnamese markets.

Serves 4

TOM YUM HED TOFU
TOFU COCONUT MILK SOUP

Coconut milk is a staple not only in Laos but also in most Asian countries. The rich flavor that coconut milk imparts to curries and soups, not to mention desserts is almost addictive. The appetizing aroma of bubbling coconut milk still reminds me of my mother's kitchen. Unless your are allergic to it I strongly recommend its use in any recipe that calls for it.

Ingredients

4 cups vegetable stock
1 can coconut milk
2 fresh chilies, cut in half lengthwise and seeded
1 stalk lemon grass, cut in half and crushed with a pestle
2 teaspoons salt
2 tablespoons fish sauce
4 kaffir lime leaves, torn in half
1 tablespoon roasted chili paste (Nam Prik Phao)
3 1/2 tablespoons lime juice
8 oz. fresh tofu, cut into 16 square pieces
1/2 cup fresh mushrooms, sliced
1/4 cup straw mushrooms
3 cherry tomatoes, halved
5 stalks of cilantro, chopped coarsely, for garnish

Preparation

In a soup pot bring vegetable stock to a boil. Add coconut milk, fresh chilies, lemon grass, salt, fish sauce, and kaffir lime leaves. Boil for 5 minutes. Add chili paste, lime juice, tofu, both kinds of mushrooms, and cherry tomatoes. Boil briefly and remove from heat. Serve in a large soup tureen garnished with chopped cilantro leaves.

Serves 4

TOM YUM GAI
HOT and SOUR CHICKEN SOUP

This soup, made with chicken or with prawns, is probably one of the most familiar and popular dishes from Laos and Thailand. If you use prawns you would call it Tom Yum Goong. Served during the hot or cold season, it is full of the warm sense of the Lao countryside.

Ingredients

4 cups chicken stock
2 fresh chilies, cut in half lengthwise and seeded
1 stalk lemon grass, cut in half and crushed with a pestle
2 teaspoons salt
2 tablespoons fish sauce
4 kaffir lime leaves
1 tablespoon roasted chili paste (Nam Prik Phao)
3 1/2 tablespoons lime juice
1/4 pound chicken breast, thinly sliced
1/2 cup sliced fresh mushrooms
1/4 cup straw mushrooms
5 stalks of cilantro, chopped coarsely, for garnish

Preparation

In a soup pot bring chicken stock to a boil. Add fresh chilies, lemon grass, salt, fish sauce, and kaffir lime leaves. Boil for 5 minutes. Add chili paste, lime juice, chicken, and both kinds of mushrooms. Boil briefly until chicken is cooked and remove from heat. Serve in a large soup tureen garnished with chopped cilantro leaves.

Serves 4

TOM KA GOONG
PRAWN COCONUT MILK SOUP

This is a light, fragrant and delicious soup that is perfect served before a substantial main course.

Ingredients

1 can of coconut milk
2 cups water
1 cup of sliced young coconut meat
4 slices fresh galangal
4 kaffir lime leaves
1 stalk lemon grass, cut in half and smashed
1 teaspoon salt
2 1/2 tablespoons fish sauce
1 teaspoon sugar
1 pound prawns, shelled and deveined
1/2 cup straw mushrooms
4 fresh mushrooms, sliced
1/3 cup of lime juice
1 tablespoon sliced green onions for garnish

Preparation

Mix coconut milk and water in a pot over medium high heat. Let boil for about 5 minutes. Add fresh coconut, galangal, kaffir lime leaves, lemon grass, salt, fish sauce and sugar. Lower heat and continue to simmer for about 15 minutes. Turn heat to high and bring back to a boil. Add prawns, mushrooms, and lime juice. Remove from heat. Serve in a large soup tureen garnished with sliced green onions.

You can substitute chicken or tofu for the prawns in this recipe.

Serves 4

KANG KAO LAO
LAO BEEF SOUP

During the war heavy bombing destroyed vast amounts of agricultural land in Laos leaving heavily damaged and dried out tracts of land. Vegetables were in very short supply since planting had been repeatedly interrupted. This soup, nick-named the "to live soup" became not only popular but also vital for urban dwellers. It was also a dietary mainstay for the students who lived in college dormitories.

Ingredients

4 cups beef stock
1/2 teaspoon ground chili
1 tablespoon soy sauce
1 tablespoon fish sauce
1/2 teaspoon salt
1 tablespoon lemon juice or vinegar
6 cherry tomatoes
1/2 pound Beef, thinly sliced
1 cup bean sprouts
1 green onion, sliced
1 tablespoon crispy garlic (sauté garlic in oil until crispy)
A pinch Black pepper

Preparation

In a soup pot bring beef stock to a boil. Add ground chili, soy sauce, fish sauce, salt, lemon juice, and cherry tomatoes. Boil briefly. Mix in beef and bean sprouts. Serve in a large soup tureen sprinkled with green onions, crispy garlic, and black pepper.

Serves 4

PAPAYA SALAD

SALADS

STRIPED BASS SALAD VIENTIANE STYLE
CRAB MEAT SALAD
BEEF SALAD
SPICY CHICKEN SALAD
PAPAYA SALAD
JUMPING SHRIMP SALAD
SPICY PRAWN SALAD
CATFISH SALAD
RAW FISH SALAD
BAMBOO SHOOT SALAD

LAAP PLA KAO
STRIPED BASS SALAD VIENTIANE STYLE

Ma kheua pro is a small Lao eggplant about the size of a ping pong ball. They are usually white with a green cap.

Ingredients

2 cups water
3 tablespoons sliced anchovy fillets
1 teaspoon salt
4 garlic cloves
3 ma kheua pro eggplants, sliced in half
1/2 pound striped bass fillet, minced
1 teaspoon dried chili powder
4 mint leaves, finely sliced
4 cilantro stalks with leaves, chopped
1 lemon grass stalk, finely sliced
1 kaffir lime leaf, finely sliced
1 green onion, finely sliced
1/2 tablespoon roasted sticky rice powder *

Fresh vegetables of your choice for serving platter, such as:
1 Head of lettuce, Romaine or iceberg
1 cucumber, sliced
2 Yard long beans, cut into 3 inch lengths
Ma kheur pro eggeplant, cut in half or sliced
Fresh chilies, whole

Preparation

In a small saucepan bring the water, anchovies and salt to a boil. Continue to boil for a few minutes. Remove from heat and transfer to a large bowl to cool.

Grill or roast the garlic and ma kheur pro over an open flame until soft. Transfer to a large mortar and pound well. Add minced bass and continue pounding until the mixture thickens. Add 1/2 of the anchovy broth and continuing pounding for about 2 minutes. Add the rest of the broth and pound for an additional 2 minutes. Add chili powder, mint, cilantro, lemon grass, kaffir lime leaf, green onion, and roasted sticky rice powder. Mix well. Pour into a dipping bowl and set in the middle of a serving platter.

Surround the dipping bowl with the sliced fresh vegetables. Serve as a dip with the fresh vegetables.

Serves 6

YUM NUER POO
CRAB MEAT SALAD

Those of you who like crab and live in a place with fresh crab will enjoy serving this easy–to–make salad to your dinner guests during crab season. If you'd like your crab salad a bit more piquant, add a couple of sliced kaffir lime leaves along with the mint and cilantro.

Ingredients

1/2 pound cooked crabmeat
2 fresh chilies, seeded and thinly sliced
1 stalk lemon grass, thinly sliced
2 shallots, thinly sliced
2 slices fresh ginger, julienned
1 celery stalk, thinly sliced
1 teaspoon sesame oil
1 1/2 tablespoons fish sauce
1 teaspoon sugar
2 tablespoons lime juice
10 mint leaves, thinly sliced
1/4 cup chopped cilantro leaves
1 green onion, thinly sliced

GRANISH
Romaine or Iceberg lettuce, Cucumber and Carrot slices

Preparation

In a large bowl combine fresh chilies, lemon grass, shallots, ginger, celery, sesame oil, fish sauce, sugar, and lime juice. Mix well. Add mint leaves, cilantro, green onion, and crab meat. Toss thoroughly. Serve on a bed of lettuce. Garnish with cucumber and carrot slices.

Serves 4

NUAR NAM TOK
BEEF SALAD

Beef salad is another very familiar dish from northern Thailand. It is an excellent savory appetizer suitable for a picnic or a sit-down dinner.

Ingredients

1 pound beef flank steak
3 tablespoons lime juice
2 1/2 tablespoons fish sauce
1 tablespoon sugar
1 stalk lemon grass, thinly sliced
2 shallots, thinly sliced
2 fresh chilies, seeded and thinly sliced
1/2 cup mint leaves
2 green onions, thinly sliced
1/2 cup chopped cilantro
1 tablespoon roasted sticky rice powder
1/2 teaspoon chili powder
1 head of iceberg or romaine lettuce

Preparation

Grill flank steak to medium rare. When cool thinly slice the steak into one-inch strips. In a large bowl combine lime juice, fish sauce, and sugar. Mix well. Add beef, lemon grass, shallots, fresh chilies, mint leaves, green onions, cilantro, chili powder and the roasted sticky rice powder. Toss well and serve on bed of lettuce.

Serves 6

LAAP GAI
SPICY CHICKEN SALAD

No discussion of Laotian cooking is complete without mentioning Laap Gai. And eating Laap Gai is even better than talking about it.

Ingredients

1 boneless and skinless chicken breast, minced
1/2 cup water
1 1/2 tablespoons fish sauce
1 teaspoon chili powder
2 fresh chilies, seeded and thinly sliced
2 tablespoons lemon juice
1 1/2 shallots, thinly sliced
1 stalk lemon grass, thinly sliced
1/2 cup chopped cilantro
1/2 cup mint leaves
2 green onions, thinly sliced
1 tablespoon roasted sticky rice powder
1 head of lettuce, washed and drained
2 ma kheua pro eggplants, cut into quarters
1/2 pound ma kheua phuang eggplants, broken into small bunches
1 cucumber, sliced

Preparation

In a saucepan cook the minced chicken with 1/2 cup of water for about 5 minutes. Remove from heat and let cool. Squeeze the liquid from the cooked chicken back into the pan and set the chicken aside. Add fish sauce to the pan and simmer until the sauce mixture thickens. Let it cool. In a mixing bowl combine the sauce with the chicken meat, chili powder, fresh chilies, lemon juice, shallots, lemon grass, cilantro, mint leaves, and green onions. Toss well. Stir in the roasted sticky rice powder. Serve on a bed of lettuce garnished with Lao eggplants and cucumber slices.

Serves 4

SOM TUM
PAPAYA SALAD

Papaya salad is eaten extensively throughout Laos. It is one of the Laotian dishes regu-
larly served at the daily family meal.

In 1998 the author, representing Dara Restaurant won the first-prize trophy for the
"BEST SOM TUM" at the Amazing Thai food Festival sponsored by the Thai Association
of Northern California.

Ingredients

2 cups shredded young, green papaya
2-4 red chili peppers
1 clove garlic
1/2 tablespoon shrimp paste
2 tablespoons fish sauce
1 1/2 tablespoons sugar
1 lime, thinly sliced
8 cherry tomatoes sliced
1 head lettuce and/or cabbage, shredded
1 tablespoon chopped peanuts (optional)

Preparation

Crush red chili peppers and garlic in the mortar pestle. Mix in the shrimp paste to
make a thick paste. In a mixing bowl mix the paste together with the fish sauce and
sugar. Toss in the shredded papaya, sliced lime, and tomatoes. Mix thoroughly.

Prepare a platter with a bed of the lettuce and/or cabbage. Spoon the som tum over
the lettuce or cabbage and top with the chopped peanuts.

Serves 4

GOONG TENT
JUMPING SHRIMP SALAD

Jumping Shrimp Salad is a well-known and favorite dish in the fishing villages along the Mekong River in Laos. Small fresh water shrimp are best in this typical Lao fishing village seafood salad, considered by some to be the best of the many excellent shrimp salads of Laos.

Jumping Shrimp Salad goes well with Lao white rice wine.

Ingredients

1/2 pound fresh water shrimp, shell, devein, remove head and tail
2 tablespoons lemon juice
1 tablespoon fish sauce
2-4 red chilies, seeded and thinly sliced
1/2 cup chopped mint leaves
2 green onions, thinly sliced
1 shallot, thinly sliced
1/2 cilantro plant, leaves, stems and roots, chopped*
2 kaffir lime leaves, thinly sliced
1 stalk lemon grass, thinly sliced
3 fresh yard long beans, sliced
1/2 tablespoon roasted sticky rice powder
1 head lettuce, romaine or iceberg

Preparation

In a large bowl combine lime juice, fish sauce, and red chilies. Soak the shrimp in the lime solution for 15 minutes. Lightly toss in the mint leaves, green onions, shallot, cilantro, kaffir lime leaves, lemon grass, yard long beans and finally the roasted sticky rice powder. Serve on a bed of lettuce.

Serves 2

* If you can not find the whole plant in the market use 6-8 whole stalks.

PA GOONG
SPICY PRAWN SALAD

This simple grilled prawn salad recipe is from Chiang Mai in northern Thailand and is very popular in both Thailand and Laos. The original recipe comes from Laos where the prawns are used raw instead of grilled.

Ingredients

1 pound mid–sized prawns, shelled and deveined
2 tablespoons lemon juice
1 tablespoon fish sauce
1 tablespoon soy bean chili paste (available in most Asian markets)
2–3 fresh chilies, seeded and sliced
5 shallots, thinly sliced
1 tablespoon thinly sliced lemon grass
1/2 cup mint leaves
1 tomato, diced
1 green onion, sliced
1 head of lettuce, romaine or iceberg

Preparation

Put prawns on bamboo skewers and grill over charcoal until medium rare. Remove prawns from skewers. In a mixing bowl mix together lemon juice, fish sauce, and soy bean chili paste. Gently toss in the prawns, chilies, shallots, lemon grass, mint leaves, tomatoes and green onion until thoroughly mixed. Serve on a bed of lettuce.

Serves 4

LAAP PA DUK
CATFISH SALAD

With its abundant ponds and rivers, and bomb craters, Laos has many delicious fresh water fish and dozens of recipes, including this all time favorite. Lapp Pla Duk has become a signature dish for Dara Restaurant in Berkeley. I know it is my publisher's favorite lunch.

Ingredients

1 cup corn oil
1 pound catfish fillet
1 lemon grass stalk, thinly sliced
1 teaspoon fresh ginger, julienned
1 shallot, thinly sliced
1/4 cup mint leaves, torn into pieces
1/4 cup sliced green onions
1/4 cup chopped cilantro
1-2 fresh red chilies, seeded and thinly sliced
1 tablespoon lemon juice
2 tablespoons fish sauce
1 tablespoon sugar
1/2 cup crispy rice, break up into chunks
1 Head of lettuce, romaine or iceberg

Preparation

In a frying pan heat oil over high heat and deep-fry catfish on both sides until golden brown. Drain on absorbent paper towels. Chop or break catfish into small pieces. In a large bowl combine lemon grass, ginger, shallot, mint leaves, green onions, cilantro, chilies, lime juice, fish sauce, sugar and catfish. Mix well. Finally toss in the broken up pieces of crispy rice. Serve on a bed of lettuce.

Serves 4

KOY PA
RAW FISH SALAD

Do not be put off by the thought of eating raw fish. The cod or striped bass in this recipe will "cook" in the marinade. The result is delicious.

Ingredients

1 pound cod or striped bass fillets, cut across the grain into thin   strips, remove any bones
1/2 cup lime juice
3 tablespoons fish sauce
6 fresh chilies, seeded and thinly sliced
15 mint leaves, chopped
6 stalks cilantro, chopped
1 stalk lemon grass, thinly sliced
2 shallots, thinly sliced
2 yard long beans, thinly sliced
2 green onions, chopped
2 teaspoon roasted sticky rice powder

Garnish:

lettuce, ma kheua pro eggplant, cucumber slices

Preparation

Put cod or striped bass strips into a bowl. Add lime juice and fish sauce and toss well. Cover and store in the refrigerator for 30 minutes. After the fish has marinated for half an hour squeeze out and save the excess liquid returning the fish to the bowl. Boil the liquid for 1 minute and set aside to cool. Pour the cooled liquid back into the bowl with the fish and add chilies, mint, cilantro, lemon grass, shallots, and green onions and yard long beans. Stir well. Serve on a bed of lettuce garnished with a variety of fresh vegetables of your choice.

Serves 4

SOUP NO MAI
BAMBOO SHOOT SALAD

The mountains of northern Laos are well known for their large, crunchy and succulent bamboo shoots. The taste of fresh bamboo shoots, sesame seeds and grilled shallots make a delicious salad that can be served either hot or cold. Bamboo shoots are available fresh and canned. Winter shoots are smaller and more tender than spring shoots. If using fresh shoots be sure to par boil and rinse well before use.

Ingredients

1/2 pound ground pork or ground chicken
1 garlic bulb, grilled or roasted
2 shallots, grilled or roasted
2 green or red chilies
1/2 teaspoon salt
1 cup of spinach juice*
1 1/2 tablespoons fish sauce
1 green onion, chopped
1 pound bamboo shoots, thinly sliced
1/4 cup chopped cilantro
1 tablespoon sesame seeds, roasted

Preparation

In a wok over high heat stir-fry ground meat until crispy. Drain off excess fat and set aside to cool.

Pound garlic, shallots, chilies, and salt in a mortar to make a paste. Place the paste in a large mixing bowl. Stir in spinach juice and fish sauce. Toss in green onion, bamboo shoots, cilantro, sesame seeds, and the ground meat. Mix well and serve.

* Purée one bunch of fresh spinach with a 1/4 cup of water or purée 1 cup of frozen spinach with 1/2 cup of water. Strain or filter through cheesecloth.

Serves 4

SEAFOOD IN SPICY SAUCE

MAIN DISHES

STUFFED PEPPERS
DEEP FRIED ROCK COD
PRAWNS ON A STICK
CRISPY EEL
STIR FRIED RICE NOODLE
STIR FRIED WATER SPINACH
CLAY BAKED FISH
STUFFED FROG
CRISPY CHICKEN WINGS
STUFFED EGGPLANT
FRIED FISH WITH GARLIC SAUCE
STEAMED VEGETABLES WITH SESAME SEEDS
SOUSI SALMON
CRISPY RICE WITH VEGETABLES
LAO RICE PILAF
POACHED SOLE WITH SPICY DILL SAUCE
RED CURRY PRAWNS
YELLOW CURRY CHICKEN
DRIED BEEF VEGETABLE STEW
GREEN CURRY HEARTS OF PALM WITH MEKONG CATFISH
STIR-FRIED PORK
STEAMED CHICKEN OVER RICE PILAF
CRISPY LEMON GRASS CHICKEN
SEAFOOD IN SPICY SAUCE
GRILLED SEA PERCH
SWEET AND SOUR LYCHEE
CASHEW NUT CHICKEN
STIR-FRIED BAMBOO SHOOTS
STEAMED CATFISH IN A BANANA LEAF
STUFFED TOMATOES IN COCONUT MILK
GOLDEN TROUT IN GREEN CURRY
PINEAPPLE FRIED RICE

YAD SAI MARPED
STUFFED PEPPERS

Capsicum Annum, is what we know as the bell pepper, sweet pepper or pimento. It is used in stir-fried dishes and makes a great receptacle for almost any type of stuffing. It is not nearly as important as hot chilies in Laotian cooking. This dish should be familiar to many of you. If I am not mistaken I think stuffed bell peppers is an American classic.

Ingredeints

6 fresh green and red large peppers or bell peppers
1/2 pound ground pork
2 shallots, thinly sliced
1 clove garlic, chopped
1 teaspoon chopped cilantro
1 teaspoon salt
Pinch black pepper
1 teaspoon soy sauce
1 teaspoon fish sauce
1 egg
1/2 cup clear noodles, soaked until soft, drained and chopped
1/2 cup dried mushrooms, soaked until soft, drained and chopped

Preparation

Cut off the tops of the bell peppers and set aside. Remove the seeds and central core from each bell pepper. Rinse, drain and pat dry. In a large bowl combine all of the remaining ingredients and mix well. Carefully stuff each bell pepper with the mixture and cover with the top. Steam for 15–20 minutes. Serve with sweet and sour sauce or sauce of choice, refer to the sauce section.

Serves 4

PA TOD LAO
DEEP FRIED ROCK COD

Lao explain the origin of this dish as follows. Leaving his wife behind to work at the mill the local miller went fishing in the millstream where he caught a fresh rock cod. He brought the fish back to his wife to cook. With the flour dust still on her hands from working hard in the mill she patted the fish before frying it. Or so the story goes.

Ingredients

1 rock cod, about one pound, sea perch can also be used
2 tablespoon tapioca flour
1/2 teaspoon salt
Oil for frying

Garnish

Lime, spring onions, lettuce, carrots, cucumbers, or tomatoes.

Preparation

Clean and wash the fish. Pat dry with paper towels. Score both sides diagonally in a diamond pattern. On a platter, mix flour and salt together. Dredge the fish through the flour. Shake off excess flour. In a wok, heat oil over high heat. When the oil is hot, deep-fry the fish on both sides until golden brown. Remove fish from oil and drain. Place it on a serving platter and garnish with fresh vegetables of your choice. Serve with Fish Hot listed in the Dipping Sauce section.

Serves 2

GOONG NANG PING
PRAWNS ON A STICK

The meat of a fresh, good quality jumbo prawn is sweet and quick cooking. Grilled prawns should be crunchy providing a perfect base for dipping in this slightly spicy sauce. Bangkok is justly famous for this dish.

Ingredients

1 pound jumbo prawns, shelled and deveined, leave the tail fan
2 tablespoons oyster sauce
2 cloves garlic, chopped
1/2 teaspoon black pepper
1 teaspoon sugar
1/2 tablespoon cilantro roots, ground
1 tablespoon oil
Bamboo skewers for grilling

Preparation

In a bowl combine oyster sauce, garlic, black pepper, sugar, cilantro, and oil. Add the prawns and mix well. Set aside to marinate. After an hour or so run a bamboo skewer through the length of each prawn. Reserve the marinade sauce. Grill prawns over a charcoal fire for 3–4 minutes on each side brushing often with the marinade. Make sure not to overcook. When the prawns are cooked, place on a platter and serve with Orange Mustard Sauce. The recipe is in the Dipping Sauce section.

Serves 4

FRESH ROLL

HEAVENLY BEEF

BAG OF GOLD

ANT EGG SOUP

SOUR PORK IN BANANA LEAF

DEEP FRIED ROCK COD

BANANA CHIPS

YOUNG COCONUT ICE CREAM

EELN KROB
CRISPY EEL

To those of you who have never eaten eel, "Don't be afraid to eat this strange fish." This recipe's straight forward approach to crispy eel is a marvelous tasting seafood treat.

Ingredients

1 pound fresh water eel fillets
5 tablespoon cornstarch
2 cloves garlic, crushed
1 teaspoon fresh, minced ginger
1 tablespoon brown sugar
1 tablespoon fish sauce
1/2 tablespoon dark soy sauce
2 – 4 fresh chilies
1/2 cup water
1/2 tablespoon oil for frying

Preparation

Cut eel fillets into 3" x 1/2" pieces. Sprinkle the pieces with salt and dredge through the cornstarch. Set aside. Heat oil in a wok to about 300 F. Deep fry the eel until crispy. Remove from the oil and drain. Pour off all but 1/2 tablespoon of the hot oil. Add garlic and ginger. Stir–fry briefly and lower the heat. Stir in the sugar, fish sauce, dark soy sauce, and fresh chilies.

Mix water with 1 1/2 teaspoons of cornstarch. Stirring constantly add cornstarch mixture to the sauce to thicken it. Return crispy eel to the wok and carefully stir to coat with the sauce. Scoop the eel onto a serving platter, coat with sesame seeds and serve. Pour remaining sauce into a bowl for dipping the eel.

Serves 4.

KOA MEE or PAD THAI
STIR FRIED RICE NOODLE

In Laos and Thailand this noodle dish is often eaten as an afternoon snack. Hat Yai in southern Thailand is well known for its pad thai.

Now that you see how easy it is to make this very popular dish at home you can try some of the more unfamiliar dishes next time you order a meal at Dara Restaurant.

Ingredients

1 bag rice noodles soaked in water until soft and drained
3 1/2 tablespoons oil
2 eggs, beaten
2 oz shrimp, shelled and deveined
1 tablespoon salted pickled radish or turnip, chopped
2 tablespoon sugar
2 1/2 tablespoons vinegar
2 tablespoons fish sauce
1/2 tablespoon paprika
2 green onions, cut into 1-inch lengths
5 oz bean sprouts, ends removed
1 tablespoon roasted peanuts, chopped

Garnish: cilantro, lettuce, lime slice, crispy dry chilies

Preparation

Heat 1 1/2 tablespoons oil in a large frying pan over medium heat. Use half of the beaten eggs and make a small omelet. Remove from the pan to cool. Slice the omelet and set aside. Heat remaining oil in the frying pan. Add the rest of the egg stirring briefly. Add shrimp, salted pickled radish, and noodles. Keep stirring until the noodles are soft. Add sugar, vinegar, fish sauce, and paprika. Stir-fry thoroughly for 1 minute. Toss in green onions, bean sprouts, and ground peanuts, stirring thoroughly once more. Arrange on a platter. Top with the sliced egg, cilantro, lettuce, and crispy dry chilies. Serve with lime slices.

Serves 4.

PAD PAK BOONG
STIR FRIED WATER SPINACH

Water spinach is also known as swamp cabbage. It is called ong choi in Chinese. If you cannot find ong choi in your local market, use spinach instead. This green is so healthy that I recommend it for daily use either stir-fried as in this recipe, in soups or in salads.

Ingredients

1 pound water spinach, cut into 2" lengths, wash and drain
2 cloves garlic, crushed
4 fresh chilies, cut in half lengthwise
1 teaspoon yellow bean sauce
pinch salt
1 teaspoon sugar
1 1/2 tablespoons oil

Preparation

Place the oil in a wok over high heat. When the oil starts to smoke add garlic and chilies. Stir briefly. Add water spinach, yellow bean sauce, sugar, and salt. Continuing stirring for a few minutes or until vegetables are soft. Empty onto a platter and serve hot.

Serves 4

PA POW
CLAY BAKED FISH

Sealing meat inside clay and baking it in a bed of coals is an old method of cooking without a pot. This might be a fun dish to try on you next fishing trip: sort of a Lao Luau. Obviously this is not a dish for your modern kitchen, as it requires a fire pit. But I suppose you could use your fireplace.

Ingredients

1 striped bass 16" long or any white fish
1 whole banana leaf 40" long cut in half
1 teaspoon salt
1 stalk lemon grass, finely chopped
2 slices fresh galanga root, chopped
2 kaffir lime leaves, cut in half
1 tablespoon fish sauce
5–6 pounds wet clay
Charcoal
Toothpicks to seal banana leaves

Preparation

Prepare a hot bed of charcoal with enough charcoal to cover the clay–enveloped fish completely.

Scale, clean, and wash the fish. Score both sides of the fish with shallow crisscross slices. Lay the banana leaves on a flat surface. Place the fish on the banana leaves so that it will be completely enclosed by the banana leaves when it is wrapped.

In a small bowl combine salt, lemon grass, galanga, kaffir lime leaves, and fish sauce. Mix well and pour over the fish. Tightly fold the banana leaves around the fish on all sides. Secure with toothpicks. Knead the clay until soft and spread it over the leaf encased fish package evenly until sealed. Bake under the charcoal for 1 hour. Carefully remove the clay and banana leaves and gently transfer the whole fish to a platter. Garnish with fresh vegetables of your choice. Serve with Clay Baked Fish Sauce. Recipe is in the Dipping Sauce section.

Serves 4

YUD SAI KOOB
STUFFED FROG

In America frog is not such a popular food. In Laos and Cambodia the people love frog: grilled, stuffed, deep-fried, it doesn't matter. I don't know whether Laos influenced the French with its love of frog's legs or the French simple reinforced the Lao's love for the dish.

Ingredients

2 medium size frogs, gutted and washed, feet removed
1 stalk lemon grass, finely chopped
2 cloves garlic, crushed
2 shallots, chopped
3 fresh chilies, seeds removed and sliced
4 oz ground pork
2 teaspoons salt
Pinch of black pepper
2 green onions, chopped
Needle and thread or
Small bamboo skewers

Preparation

In a bowl, combine 1 tablespoon of salt with 2 quarts of cold water. Soak the cleaned frogs in the brine for 5 to 10 minutes. Meanwhile, pound the lemon grass, garlic, shallots and chilies well in a mortar and pestle to form a paste. Add the ground pork, salt, black pepper, and green onions. Mix well. Remove the frogs from the brine, drain and pat dry with paper towels. Stuff the frogs with the ground pork mixture and seal with thread or small bamboo skewers. Steam in a steamer for 30 minutes. Remove from steamer and grill over medium heat until golden brown. Serve with sticky rice and garlic sauce. See sauce section for recipe.

Serves 4

KO GAI TOD
CRISPY CHICKEN WINGS

Gai (sometimes written, kai) is chicken in Lao as well as Chinese. And like the Chinese they eat almost every part of this noble fowl, including the feet and the partially incubated eggs. The respect that the Lao have for chicken meat approaches reverence. It is one of the symbolic foods used in the informal spirit worship ceremony known as baçi. Although turkeys have been introduced into Laos they are too large an animal for most Lao recipes and could never replace the chicken in popularity.

Ingredients

1/2 pound chicken wings, cut at the joint
2 tablespoons all purpose flour
1 teaspoon salt
1 teaspoon sugar
1 teaspoon coriander seed, powdered
Pinch of black pepper
1 tablespoon sesame seeds, toasted
1 clove garlic, minced
1 egg, beaten
4 cups of oil

Preparation

In a large bowl, combine flour, salt, sugar, coriander seed powder, black pepper, sesame seeds, garlic, and egg. Mix well. Add chicken wings and thoroughly coat with the mixture. Set aside. Place the oil in a wok over high heat. When the oil is hot deep fry chicken wings until crisp and golden brown. Remove and drain. Serve with Chicken Hot Sauce. See Dipping Sauce section for recipe.

Serves 4

YAD SAI MAKEUN
STUFFED EGGPLANT

Although Laos has a few varieties of unusual eggplants this recipe calls for the standard long eggplant. For a more complete explanation of eggplants look in the glossary.

Ingredients

2 Asian eggplants, long ones not round ones
1/2 pound catfish cut into 1-inch squares
4 pieces bacon cut into 1-inch squares
1/2 teaspoon salt
1 egg
1 cup all purpose flour
1 cup water
2 cloves garlic, crushed
1 teaspoon red chili paste
1 tablespoon fish sauce
1 teaspoon sugar
4 fresh chilies, seeds removed and sliced
15 sweet basil buds (just the tips)
2 cups oil

Preparation

Slice the eggplant into half-inch lengths. Partially slice each eggplant piece to form a round sandwich. Place a slice of catfish and bacon inside each sandwich.

Beat salt, egg, flour, and 1/2 cup of water into a smooth batter, adding more water if necessary.

Heat oil in a wok over high heat. When the oil is hot, dip each piece of stuffed eggplant into the batter and deep fry until golden brown. Remove and drain.

Pour off all but a small amount of the oil. Briefly sauté garlic and red chili paste. Add water, fish sauce, sugar, and fresh chilies. Stir well. Toss in the deep-fried stuffed eggplant and basil buds. Serve warm.

SERVES 4

PA TOD KATEAM
FRIED FISH WITH GARLIC SAUCE

Although my mother used to make this dish with baby carp almost any very small fish will do. Smelt or white fish fingerlings are a good substitute.

Ingredients

1 pound fish fingerlings
1 tablespoon salt
1 cup all purpose flour
1/2 cup water
1 small tomato for garnish

Preparation

Prepare the Garlic Sauce according to the recipe in the Dipping Sauce section

Sift the flour and salt into a deep mixing bowl. Gradually stir in enough water to make a very thick batter. Heat oil to 365º F in a deep frying pan. When the oil is hot, take 3 fish at a time, pressing the tails together firmly to make a fan shape, and gently dip them into the batter. Carefully lower the "fish fan" into the hot oil. Deep-fry until crisp and golden. Remove from the hot oil and drain. Continue in the same way with the remaining fish. Arrange the fish on a platter with the sliced tomato and serve with Garlic Sauce.

Serves 6

CHOUP PAK HOT JENGLE
STEAMED VEGETABLES WITH SESAME SEEDS

This dish originally comes from Northern Laos and goes well with sticky rice. It is an unusual and appetizing way to serve your favorite vegetables at a family meal.

Ingredients

1 pound fresh vegetables of choice, cut into 1 inch pieces, i.e.
  turnip, squash, sponge gourd, ong choi, green beans.
6 Dried Chinese black mushrooms soaked in water and sliced
1/2 cup of Ma Keua Phuang (small Thai eggplant, cut in half
3 yard long beans cut into 1 inch lengths
2 cloves garlic, crushed
4 slices fresh ginger
3 dried chilies, seeded and roasted over an open flame
2 tablespoons fish sauce
2 teaspoons sesame seeds, roasted
1/2 cup of cilantro, chopped
2 green onions, sliced

Preparation

Wash and drain vegetables. Steam vegetables, except green onions, and black mush-rooms for 10 minutes. Place steamed ingredients in a large bowl to cool.

With a mortar and pestle, or food processor, grind garlic, ginger and dried chilies into a paste. Stir the garlic and ginger paste into the large bowl of vegetables. Toss the fish sauce, cilantro and green onions into the bowl and mix gently. Sprinkle the sesame seeds on top and serve cold.

Serves 4

SOUSI PA SALMON
SOUSI SALMON

In my hometown it is said that a local woman named Sousi created this dish, but to this day no one knows who she was.

Ingredients

1 pound salmon fillet
1 tablespoon red curry paste
2 cups coconut milk
2 kaffir lime leaves, finely sliced
1 tablespoon pineapple juice
1 tablespoon fish sauce
1 teaspoon salt
2 tablespoons palm sugar
1 tomato, sliced for garnish

Preparation

In a pan over medium heat, stir–fry curry paste for 2 minutes. Add coconut milk and simmer until fragrant. Stir in pineapple juice, fish sauce, salt, palm sugar, and kaffir lime leaves. Add salmon and simmer for about 10 minutes. Carefully remove salmon from pan and set on a serving platter. Continue to simmer the curry sauce until it thickens. Pour curry sauce over salmon and garnish with tomato slices.

Serves 4

KAO KOB PAD PAK
CRISPY RICE WITH VEGETABLES

In the old days rice was normally cooked in a clay pot. After the rice was scooped out, a layer of rice stuck to the bottom of the pot. This layer was the origin of crispy rice. This pot rice needs to be deep-fried to turn into crispy rice. Next time you have rice cooked in a clay pot scrape off some of the rice that sticks to the bottom. It is chewy and has absorbed the flavor of the various ingredients used in the recipe. Crispy rice is now made commercially and is available in most Asian markets.

Ingredients

8 crispy rice cakes (packages are available in Asian markets)
3 slices fresh ginger
1 stalk Chinese celery, cut into 1 inch lengths
6 dried shiitake mushrooms, soak until soft and slice
1/2 cup of straw mushrooms
10 snow pea pods
1/4 yellow onion, sliced
1/2 carrot, sliced
3 oz tofu, diced
1 teaspoon sesame oil
1 teaspoon salt
1 teaspoon sugar
1 tablespoon cornstarch
1 cups of water
1 1/2 tablespoons corn oil

Preparation

In a small bowl combine sesame oil, salt, sugar, water, and cornstarch. Mix well and set aside.

Heat the corn oil in a wok over medium heat. Sauté ginger and celery briefly. Add shiitake mushrooms, straw mushrooms, snow peas, yellow onion, carrot, and tofu. Continue to sauté until vegetables are cooked, about 5 minutes. Add the sauce and stir-fry until all ingredients are well combined.

Place the crispy rice cakes on a serving platter. Pour the hot vegetables over the crispy rice and serve.

Serves 4

KAO MAN LAO
LAO RICE PILAF

Pilaf most likely came to Laos via India. Pilaf is a Turkish and Urdu word meaning cooked rice. In Persian pilaw means boiled rice and meat. Today pilaf or pillau refers to rice cooked in stock with spices and meat or vegetables.

Ingredients

2 tablespoons oil
1/2 yellow onion, chopped
2 cloves garlic, minced
1 cup uncooked, long grain rice
2 1/2 cups of chicken broth
1 teaspoon soy sauce
1 tablespoon thinly sliced ginger
1/2 teaspoon red pepper flakes
1 teaspoon salt
1/3 cup sliced green onions

Preparation

In a 2–3 quart sauce pan sauté chopped onions and garlic in oil over medium heat until onions are soft. Add rice, chicken broth, soy sauce, ginger, pepper flakes, and salt. Bring to a boil, stirring once or twice. Reduce the heat. Cover and simmer 15 minutes or until rice is tender and liquid is absorbed. Remove from heat. Cover and let stand for 5 minutes. Transfer to a platter sprinkle with green onions and serve.

Serves 4

PA NYANG PAK SHEE
POACHED SOLE WITH SPICY DILL SAUCE

In Lao cooking dill is most often used in fish dishes. Alan Davidson writes that the dill in Laos is the same species as in Europe and the Near East but different to the dill of India and Indonesia.

Ingredients

1 1/2 pounds fresh sole fillets
1/2 tablespoon oil
3 cups of chicken broth
1 clove garlic, chopped
1/2 teaspoon salt
2–4 fresh chilies, sliced
1/2 tablespoon fish sauce
2 tablespoons lime juice
1 tablespoon cornstarch
3 tablespoons fresh dill, snipped from stem

Preparation

In a shallow pan bring 2 cups of chicken broth to a boil over medium–high heat. Lower heat and add fish to the pan. Simmer for 3–4 minutes or until fish is cooked. Carefully remove the fish with a slotted spoon and arrange on a warm serving platter.

In a saucepan heat the oil over medium heat. Add garlic and sauté briefly. Add the last cup of chicken broth, salt, chilies, fish sauce, lime juice, and cornstarch. Bring the mixture to a boil stirring constantly until mixture thickens. Boil 1 minute. Stir in dill. Spoon sauce over fish. Garnish as desired and serve.

Serves 6

KANG DEANG GOONG
RED CURRY PRAWNS

Recipes for curry pastes are in the curry paste section of this book. If you don't have the time or the inclination to prepare your own paste you can find tinned curry pastes in most Asian markets. Left over curry paste should keep for about 3 to 4 months in the refrigerator if you store it in a sealed glass jar.

Ingredients

1/2 pound prawns, shelled and deveined
2 1/2 cups coconut milk
1 tablespoon red curry paste
3 kaffir lime leaves, sliced
1/2 cup pineapple chunks
1/2 cup shredded young bamboo shoots
1/2 teaspoon salt
1 1/2 tablespoons fish sauce
1 tablespoon sugar
10 cherry tomatoes
2 fresh chilies, broken in half
15 sweet basil leaves

Preparation

In a saucepan over high heat combine 1 cup of coconut milk and the red curry paste. Stir constantly until the mixture bubbles. Add the remaining 1 1/2 cups of coconut milk, kaffir lime leaves, pineapple chunks, bamboo shoots, salt, fish sauce, and sugar. Lower the heat to medium and simmer until the sauce thickens. Add prawns, cherry tomatoes, fresh chilies, and sweet basil. Continue simmering until the prawns are cooked. Remove from heat and serve.

Serves 2

KANG KARI GAI
YELLOW CURRY CHICKEN

This curry recipe is good with other main ingredients as well. You can substitute firm or deep-fried tofu or gluten for the chicken and you will have a very delicious vegetarian yellow curry. Don't forget to use soy sauce instead of fish sauce if you want to make this a pure vegetarian dish. Adding kabocha squash is another vegetarian alternative.

Ingredients

2 chicken legs cut into pieces
2 chicken breasts cut into pieces
1 1/2 cans coconut milk
1 1/2 tablespoons yellow curry paste
1 teaspoon salt
2 cups water
2 potatoes, peeled and cut into pieces
1 carrot, peeled and cut into cubes
3 tablespoons fish sauce
3 tablespoons palm sugar
1/2 yellow onion, cut into cubes
1 1/2 teaspoon turmeric powder*

Preparation

In a pot over medium heat bring the coconut milk to a boil. Add yellow curry paste and stir well for about 5 minutes. Add chicken and salt. Immediately after it return to a boil add water, potatoes, carrots, fish sauce, palm sugar, yellow onion, and turmeric powder. Lower the heat and simmer about 20 minutes or until chicken is thoroughly cooked. Serve with rice and cucumber salad.

*Dry roast the turmeric before adding to the curry. This helps release the aroma and reduces its bitterness.

Serves 4

LAM SHINHANG
DRIED BEEF VEGETABLE STEW

This is originally a Northern Laos style dish. It goes well with sticky rice. For instructions on how to prepare the dried beef see "Heavenly Beef" recipe in the Appetizer section of this cookbook.

Ingredients

1/2 pound dried beef cut into 1 inch strips, see above
3 slices fresh galangal root
1 lemon grass stalk, sliced
2 kaffir lime leaves
2 tablespoons fish sauce
1/2 teaspoon salt
20 Makeur Phuang eggplant
5 Ma kheur pro eggplant, cut in half
2 Japanese eggplants, sliced lengthwise and cut into 1" pieces
5 yard-long beans, cut into 1 inch lengths
1/2 sponge gourd, sliced into 1 inch lengths
5 one-inch slices of white turnip, quartered
3 dried shiitake mushrooms, soaked in water and cut into squares
4 fresh chilies, sliced
20 sweet basil leaves
4 cups water

Preparation

In a pot over high heat bring water to a boil. Add beef, galangal, lemon grass, kaffir lime leaves, fish sauce, salt, and Japanese eggplant. Continue to boil for 15 minutes. Add yard-long beans, sponge gourd turnip, and mushrooms. Continue to boil for 5 minutes more. Lower the heat and simmer until all vegetables are cooked.

Meanwhile place chilies, Makeur Phuang, and Ma kheur pro eggplants into a mortar and crush them with a pestle until a smooth paste is formed. Scrape this mixture into the pot and mix well. Add basil, remove from heat and serve.

Serves 6

KEANG KEO YOT MAPAO ON SAI PAL DUK
GREEN CURRY HEARTS OF PALM WITH MEKONG CATFISH

Since a large area of Laos sits along the banks of the Mekong River we use its catfish for this dish. Since Mekong catfish is not readily available outside of Southeast Asia you should use whatever catfish is available in your area. Mahi mahi, sea bass, or sea perch can also be substituted for Mekong catfish.

Ingredients

1/2 pound catfish fillets cut into pieces
1 1/2 tablespoons green curry paste
3 cups coconut milk
1 cup water
1/2 teaspoon salt
2 tablespoons fish sauce
1 tablespoon palm sugar
2 kaffir lime leaves, torn
20 Ma kheua phuang eggplants
4 Ma kheua pro eggplants
2 long yard beans cut into 1-inch lengths
1 cup hearts of palm, sliced
15 sweet basil tips

Preparation

Mix 1 cup of coconut milk and the green curry paste together in a saucepan over high heat. Stir well until green curry becomes fragrant. Reduce heat. Add the re-maining 2 cups of coconut milk, 1 cup of water, salt, fish sauce, palm sugar, and kaffir lime leaves and bring to a boil. Boil for 10 minutes. Add fish and eggplants and sim-mer for 10 minutes. Add yard long beans, hearts of palm, and sweet basil. Bring back to a boil and remove from heat. Pour into a serving bowl and serve with sticky rice.

* 2 Chinese eggplants can be substituted for the 20 ma kheua phuang and 4 ma kheua pro eggplants.

Serves 4

MOO KIO
STIR-FRIED PORK

Moo is pork in Lao and it is without a doubt the most popular meat in Laos and the rest of Asia for that matter. As with the chicken we eat almost all parts of the pig. Pig trotter and tripe are very popular in my country. We also love fried pork skin and fat back. Many Lao who settled in the southern part of the United States were pleasantly surprised to find easily available fried pork rinds in their newly adopted country.

Ingredients

1/2 pound sliced pork shoulder or pork butt
2 tablespoons oil
4 cloves garlic, minced
1/2 teaspoon turmeric powder
1/2 teaspoon salt
1 tablespoon brown sugar
1/2 tablespoon soy sauce
1 tablespoon fish sauce
1 tablespoon red chili paste
2 kaffir lime leaves, thinly sliced
Lettuce and tomato for garnish

Preparation

In a wok over medium-high heat add oil and sauté garlic until fragrant. Add turmeric, pork, salt, brown sugar, soy sauce, fish sauce, and chili paste. Stir well until pork is cooked. Serve on a platter sprinkled with kaffir lime leaves. Garnish with lettuce and sliced tomatoes.

Serves 4

KAO MAN GAI
STEAMED CHICKEN OVER RICE PILAF

This recipe calls for coriander root as do many Lao and Thai dishes. Most fresh coriander available in the markets in the West is sold without the roots. So you might not
have an easy time finding the roots unless you grow it yourself. If you can find it use it
for it does impart a unique flavor. If you can't find the root, substitute a teaspoon or
two of roasted and ground coriander seeds.

Ingredients

Half a chicken, about 2 pounds
3 coriander roots, crushed
1 teaspoon salt
1 1/2 cups of uncooked, long grain rice, washed
1 tablespoon chopped yellow onion
1 tablespoon fresh ginger, thinly sliced
2 tablespoons oil
1 cucumber, sliced

Preparation

In a large pot over high heat combine 4 cups of water, coriander roots and salt and
bring to a boil. Add chicken and reduce heat to medium-low, cover the pot and
simmer for 30 minutes. In order to get a clear broth make sure to simmer the chicken
at low heat. Do not bring to a rolling boil. After chicken is cooked remove from the
pot, and set aside to cool. After the chicken is cool enough to handle chop into small
pieces. Filter 1 1/2 cups of the broth into a rice cooking pot. Any remaining chicken
broth can be stored in the refrigerator for later use. Add the rice and cook until the
rice is done and the broth is fully absorbed.

Sauté onions and ginger with oil in a wok until golden brown. Add the cooked rice
and stir-fry briefly. Transfer the rice to a serving platter. Lay the chicken on the bed
of rice. Serve with Soy Bean Ginger Sauce and sliced cucumber. See Sauce section
for sauce recipe.

Serves 2

GAI TA KHAI KROB
CRISPY LEMON GRASS CHICKEN

Originally from Southeast Asia, the citrus flavor of lemon grass is delicious with chicken. It is widely used in Thailand and Viet Nam as well as in Laos. If you can't find really fresh lemon grass stalks peel the tougher outer layers from the stalk before you slice it for this recipe. The outer layers of the stalk can be used to make tea. As with ginger we believe that lemon grass is good for the stomach.

Ingredients

1 pound boneless chicken breast, sliced
1 cup oil
2 stalks lemon grass, thinly sliced
2 shallots, thinly sliced
3 cloves garlic, chopped
1/2 teaspoon salt
1 tablespoon soy sauce
1 tablespoon palm sugar
4 dried chilies
1 tablespoon fish sauce
1/4 teaspoon black pepper

Preparation

In a wok with oil over high heat deep-fry lemon grass until golden brown. Remove from oil and drain on paper towels. Pour off all but about 1 tablespoon of the oil. Add shallots and garlic and sauté briefly. Add chicken and stir-fry about 3 minutes. Add salt, soy sauce, palm sugar, dry chilies, fish sauce, and black pepper stirring until chicken is cooked. Serve on a platter sprinkled with deep-fried lemon grass.

Serves 4

PAD PHED TALAY
SEAFOOD IN SPICY SAUCE

As in all of the recipes how hot and spicy you like your food will determine the number of chilies you use. As you all know different chilies have different levels of hotness. Use you own judgement. When I make this dish I use 8 chilies so if you like it hot use the full amount.

Ingredients

2 tablespoon cooking oil
8 fresh chilies
4 oz sea perch, deep-fried and sliced
4 oz prawns, shelled and deveined
4 oz mussels, in shells, scrubbed and cleaned
4 oz squid, cleaned, sliced into pieces
4 oz cooked crab meat
4 oz fish balls
4 oz fish cake
1/2 cup of water
1/2 yellow onion, sliced
1 zucchini, or sponge gourd, sliced
1 1/2 tablespoons fish sauce
1/2 tablespoon red chili paste
1 tablespoon sugar
1/2 teaspoon salt
1/2 cup of sweet basil, deep-fry to make crispy

Preparation

Heat the oil in a wok over medium heat and briefly stir-fry fresh chilies. Add sea perch, prawns, mussels, squid, crab meat, fish balls, fish cake, and water. Cover and cook for a few minutes or until mussel shells open. Discard the unopened mussels. Add onions, zucchini or sponge gourd, fish sauce, chili paste, salt, and sugar. Stir-fry thoroughly and transfer to a platter. Sprinkle crispy basil over the top and serve with rice.

Serves 4

PING PA
GRILLED SEA PERCH

The Lao word for fish is pa. Besides the Mekong River fish abound in streams, irrigation canals, lakes, ponds and even in the rice fields. We love fish: dinner, lunch or breakfast.

Ping Pa is best served with sticky rice. When we serve ping pa for breakfast it reminds us of the continuing Laotian cultural influences on our daily lives.

Ingredients

1 whole sea perch, about 1 to 1 1/2 pounds
1 lemon grass stalk, sliced
2 cloves garlic
4 red chilies
2 shallots
3 cilantro roots
2 green onions, chopped
1/2 teaspoon salt
Bamboo skewers
BBQ stove
Charcoal for grilling

Preparation

Scale, clean, and wash sea perch. Fillet the perch leaving the two sides joined along the belly.

In a pestle and mortar crush the lemon grass. Add garlic, chilies, shallots, cilantro root, green onions, and salt. Pound well into a paste. Spread the paste all over the inside of the sea perch. Fold the fish back together and close the cut belly side with bamboo skewers. Grill both sides slowly over a low charcoal fire until golden brown.

Serves 2

PREOWAN LYCHEE
SWEET AND SOUR LYCHEE

Logan can be substituted for lychee as a variation of this refreshing vegetarian sweet and sour dish. This is a wonderful vegetable dish on those hot days when you don't want a heavy course on the menu. If you use fresh lychee or logan don't forget to remove the seeds before cooking.

Ingredients

1 pound fresh lychee meat or 1 can lychee fruit
1/2 cup each green and red bell peppers, diced
1/2 cup pineapple chunks
1/2 potato, diced
1/2 carrot, diced
1/2 yellow onion, diced
1/2 cucumber, diced
4 cherry tomatoes
4 tablespoons ketchup
1 teaspoon salt
2 tablespoons palm sugar
2 tablespoons rice vinegar
1/2 cup of water
1/2 teaspoon black pepper
1 tablespoon corn oil
1 green onion, sliced

Preparation

Heat oil in a wok over medium-high heat. Sauté green and red bell peppers, pine-apple, potatoes, carrots, yellow onions, cucumbers, cherry tomatoes, and lychees until potatoes and carrots are cooked. In a small bowl combine ketchup, salt, palm sugar, rice vinegar and water. Add to the wok, mix well, season with salt and pepper. Remove to a serving platter and sprinkle with sliced green onions. Serve with rice.

Serves 4

HIMAPAN GAI
CASHEW NUT CHICKEN

Cashew nut chicken just might be America's all time favorite Chinese dish. While the Chinese version tends to be a bit bland the Lao version is a lot livelier and full flavored.

Ingredients

1 pound boneless chicken breast, sliced
2 cloves garlic, sliced
1/2 cup yellow onions, sliced
1 tablespoon oyster sauce
1 1/2 teaspoons dark soy sauce
Pinch salt
1/2 cup of water
8 dry chilies, fried
1/2 cup roasted cashew nuts
1 green onion, chopped
1 tablespoon oil

Preparation

Heat oil in a wok over medium heat. Sauté garlic and yellow onions briefly. Add chicken breast and sauté until chicken is cooked.
In a small bowl combine oyster sauce, dark soy sauce, salt and water. Stir into the wok with the chicken. Add fried chilies, cashew nuts, and green onions. Mix well and serve with rice.

Serves 4

PAD MOO MAI
STIR-FRIED BAMBOO SHOOTS

Of the more than 100 varieties of bamboo in Asia only about ten types have edible shoots. The crunchy texture and slightly acidic flavor of bamboo shoots make a refreshing addition to any meal. Canned shoots are more readily available than fresh or pickled ones. Fresh bamboo shoots contain a toxin that can be gotten rid of by blanching for 5 minutes. Rinse them well before using. Pickled shoots are fermented in a vinegar brine with red chili and can be a bit sour. They should be soaked in water before using. Anchovy paste adds another dimension to this dish but it might be a bit overbearing for many western palates so use sparingly.

Ingredients

1/2 pound steamed bamboo shoots
2 tablespoons salad oil
4 garlic cloves, chopped
8 fresh chilies, seeded and smashed
1 teaspoon anchovy paste
1 tablespoon green onions, minced

Preparation

Wash the steamed bamboo shoots well and drain. Heat oil in a wok over medium heat. Sauté garlic until crispy and golden brown. Scoop the garlic out of the wok leaving the oil. Add chilies, bamboo shoots, anchovy paste and green onions. Stir-fry briefly and put on a serving platter. Sprinkle with crispy garlic and serve with rice.

Serves 2

HO MOOK PA
STEAMED CATFISH IN A BANANA LEAF

This catfish recipe has been in my family for generations. It is authentic Lao. Easy to prepare it will surely impress your friends with your Lao cooking knowledge. Small slices of lemon and lime arranged on the serving platter add a nice touch and taste to this traditional fish dish. The large leaves of collard greens are a good substitute if you can't find fresh banana leaves.

Ingredients

1/2 pound catfish, cut into 1" squares
4 fresh chilies
4 shallots, chopped
2 garlic cloves, chopped
1 slice fresh galangal root
1 lemon grass stalk, sliced
1/2 teaspoon fish sauce
1 teaspoon anchovy paste
2 kaffir lime leaves, sliced
10 sweet basil leaves, chopped
1 banana leaf, cut into quarters
toothpicks to secure banana leaf

Preparation

Using a pestle and mortar or a food processor prepare a paste of the chilies, shallots, garlic, galagal and lemon grass. Add the fish sauce, anchovy paste, kaffir lime leaves, and sweet basil. Mix well. In a large bowl coat the fish fillets with the paste. Divide into 4 portions and wrap each portion in a banana leaf. Secure with toothpicks and steam over high heat for 20–25 minutes. Serve with rice.

Serves 2

YUD SAI MAR LEURN
STUFFED TOMATOES IN COCONUT MILK

Although not indigenous to Asia tomatoes have been fully incorporated into Asian cuisine as have potatoes and chili peppers, two other imports from South America. In fact chilies are so identified with most Asian styles of cooking that it is impossible to imagine what the food would have been like before the introduction of capsicum pepper by the early Spanish and Portuguese traders.

Ingredients

4 large red tomatoes
1/2 pound ground chicken or lean pork
2 tablespoons clear noodles, chopped
2 tablespoons ear mushrooms, soak in water until soft and slice
2 shallots, minced
1/2 tablespoon black pepper
1 tablespoon sugar
2 pinches of salt
1 teaspoon fish sauce
1 teaspoon soy sauce
1 egg, beaten
2 fresh chilies, seeded and cut lengthwise
1/2 can coconut milk or 7 oz of fresh coconut milk

Preparation

Cut off the tops of the tomatoes and set aside. Remove the seeds and center pulp from each tomato. Rinse, drain and pat dry. In a large bowl combine all of the remaining ingredients, except for the coconut milk, one pinch of salt and the fresh chilies and mix well. Carefully stuff each tomato with the mixture and cover with the top. Steam for 15–20 minutes.

COCONUT MILK SAUCE

Preparation

Combine coconut milk and a pinch of salt in a small pan. Bring to a boil and remove from heat. Spoon the coconut sauce on a serving plate and place the stuffed tomatoes in the center. Decorate with fresh chilies.

Serves 4

KE
O WAM PA NAI KAM
GOLDEN TROUT IN GREEN CURRY

If you can not find golden trout in your market rainbow trout will do. Salmon fillets can also be substituted.

Ingredients

1 medium size golden trout
1/2 can coconut milk
1 lemon grass stalk, smashed
2 kaffir lime leaves, broken
A pinch of salt
2 fresh chilies, broken
1 tablespoon green curry paste
1 teaspoon fish sauce
1 teaspoon sugar

Preparation

Scale, clean, wash, and pat dry the fish. In a saucepan over low heat combine the coconut milk, lemon grass, kaffir lime leaves, and salt. Bring to a simmer and add the fish. Continue to simmer until the fish is cooked. Remove the fish from the pan and place it on a serving platter. Lower the heat on the coconut milk mixture remaining in the pan. Add green curry paste and chilies. Stir until fragrant. Add fish sauce and sugar. Stir and remove from heat. Pour curry sauce over the fish and serve with rice.

Serves 2

KAO PAD MAR NATT
PINEAPPLE FRIED RICE

This is a very festive way to serve fried rice. It is very easy and looks quite fancy. Feel free to add chopped vegetables of your choice to the mix.

Ingredients

1 teaspoon oil
1 egg
1/2 pound fresh crab meat
2 fresh chilies, seeded and sliced
2 cups cooked long grain white rice
1/2 teaspoon fish sauce
1 teaspoon soy sauce
1 tablespoon sugar
A pinch of black pepper
1 green onion, chopped
1 fresh pineapple, cut in half length-wise and hollowed out
1 cup diced pineapple flesh
1 tablespoon crispy fried garlic

Preparation

Heat the oil in a skillet over high heat. Add egg and stir briefly. Add crab meat, chilies, and rice. Continue to stir and add fish sauce, soy sauce, sugar, and pepper. Mix well. Stir in green onions and diced pineapple and remove from heat. Scoop the fried rice into the scooped out pineapple shells, garnish with crispy garlic and serve.

Serves2

HOT AND SWEET SAUCE WITH GREEN MANGOES

DIPPING SAUCES

Lao people love to dip vegetables and sticky rice into a variety of hot and spicy dips. The Lao word for sauce is jéo. As you will discover from reading the recipes in my cookbook many Lao dishes involve the use of a dipping sauce. In fact in some of the recipes the main dish itself is a dip. These recipes are in the appetizer section.

Listed in this section are the various dipping sauces called for throughout the cook-book. I have added a few extra Lao sauces that you also might like to try out with some of your favorite finger foods. The name of most of the sauces is the same as for the dish with which it is used. The following sauces are listed in the order that they appear in the cookbook.

I'll start off with the recipe for one of the basic Lao dipping sauces, jéo som. This sauce is not always made the same way by each cook. Here is my version.

JÉO SOM SAUCE
DEEP FRIED QUAIL SAUCE
EGG ROLL DIPPING SAUCE #1
EGG ROLL DIPPING SAUCE #2
BAG OF GOLD HOT SAUCE
MANGO CHILI DIP
FRESH SPINACH WRAP SAUCE
SWEET AND SOUR SAUCE
MARMALADE SAUCE
HOT AND SWEET SAUCE
CUCUMBER PEANUT SALAD SAUCE
NAM LAO TAMARIND SAUCE
SPICY SATAY SAUCE
PEANUT SAUCE
FISH HOT SAUCE
CLAY BAKED FISH SAUCE
ORANGE MUSTARD SAUCE
CHICKEN HOT SAUCE
GARLIC SAUCE
SPICY DILL SAUCE
SOY BEAN GINGER SAUCE
FERMENTED SOY BEAN SAUCE
SWEET CHILI SAUCE
SWEET CHILI PEANUT SAUCE

JÉO SOM SAUCE

Ingredients

4 fresh chilies
2 cloves garlic
1 oz fish sauce
2 tablespoons fresh lemon juice
1/2 teaspoon sugar
3 stalks fresh cilantro, leaves removed and chopped

Preparation

In a pestle and mortar pound chilies and garlic together until you have a paste. Add the fish sauce, lemon juice and sugar and mix well. Pour into a small bowl and sprinkle the cilantro leaves over the top.

DEEP FRIED QUAIL SAUCE

Ingredients

2 tablespoons lime juice
1 tablespoon fish sauce
1 teaspoon sugar
1 teaspoon cilantro, chopped

Preparation

Combine all the ingredients in a bowl. Mix well and serve with Deep Fried Quail

EGG ROLL DIPPING SAUCE #1

Ingredients

1/4 cup lime juice
1/4 cup boiled water
3 tablespoons sugar
2 tablespoons ground peanuts
1/2 teaspoon salt
1/2 tablespoon finely pounded fresh chili
1 tablespoon fish sauce

Preparation

Combine all ingredients in a bowl. Mix well and serve.

EGG ROLL DIPPING SAUCE #2

Ingredients

1/4 cup vinegar
1/4 cup water
1/2 cup sugar
1/2 teaspoon salt
1/2 tablespoon well pounded fresh chili
2 teaspoons tapioca flour mixed in 2 tablespoons water

Preparation

In a small pan mix the vinegar, water, sugar, salt, and chili together. Bring to a boil. Add enough of the tapioca flour and water mixture to thicken to desired consistency. Boil for 3 – 4 minutes. Remove from heat and serve.

BAG OF GOLD HOT SAUCE

Ingredients

2–6 fresh chilies, ground (depending on degree of hotness desired)
4 garlic cloves, very finely minced
1 tablespoon salt
3 tablespoons vinegar
2 teaspoons Sugar
1 tablespoon fish sauce

Preparation

Combine ingredients and mix well. Place in a small bowl and serve.

MANGO CHILI DIP

Ingredients

2–4 fresh chilies (depending on degree of hotness desired)
1 teaspoon shrimp paste
2 cloves garlic
2 teaspoon sugar
1 1/2 tablespoons fish sauce
1/4 cup boiling water
2 young, green mangoes, julienned

Preparation

Pound the fresh chilies in a motar and pestle. Add shrimp paste, garlic, and sugar. Continue pounding until the ingredients become a paste. Add fish sauce, hot water, and mangoes. Mix well and transfer to a small bowl. Serve with Crispy Sea Perch

FRESH SPINACH WRAP SAUCE

Ingredients

1 tablespoon oil
1 garlic clove, minced
1/2 cup water
1/2 teaspoon shrimp paste
1 tablespoon sugar
1 teaspoon fish sauce

Preparation

In a small pan sauté the garlic in oil over high heat until golden brown. Add water, shrimp paste, brown sugar, and fish sauce. Stir well; remove from heat and pour into a small bowl to cool. Serve with Fresh Spinach Wrap.

SWEET AND SOUR SAUCE

Ingredients

1/2 cup tomato catsup
1/4 cup shredded fresh young ginger
1 tablespoon vinegar
1 tablespoon sugar
1 teaspoon salt
1/2 teaspoon ground black pepper

Preparation

Mix all ingredients together in a pot and bring to a boil. Simmer for 15 minutes and serve.

MARMALADE SAUCE

Ingredients

1/4 cup orange marmalade
1/4 cup vinegar
1/4 teaspoon salt

Preparation

Mix all ingredients in a pot. Stir the ingredients over medium heat just long enough to mix well. Serve

HOT AND SWEET SAUCE

Ingredients

1/4 cup water
3 tablespoons fish sauce
1/2 teaspoon soy sauce
1/2 cup Palm sugar
10 shallots, finely sliced
4 fresh chilies, seeded and chopped
1/4 cup dried shrimp, ground

Preparation

Heat the water in a pot. Add fish sauce, soy sauce, and palm sugar. Mix well and boil until mixture thickens. Set aside to cool. After mixture has cooled add shallots and fresh chilies and dried shrimp. Pour into a small serving bowl.

CUCUMBER PEANUT SAUCE

Ingredients

1/3 cup vinegar
2 tablespoons sugar
1 teaspoon salt
2 shallots, minced
1 red chili, thinly sliced
1 tablespoon chopped, roasted peanuts
1 tablespoon chopped fresh cilantro
Sliced cucumbers

Preparation

In a saucepan heat the vinegar, sugar, salt, shallots and chili stirring constantly until sugar dissolves. When the mixture comes to a boil remove from heat. Mix in peanuts and pour into a serving bowl. Garnish with chopped cilantro and serve with sliced cucumbers.

NAM LAO TAMARIND SAUCE

Ingredients

3 cloves garlic, minced
2 shallots, minced
1 tablespoon oil
1/2 cup tamarind juice
1 1/2 tablespoons oyster sauce
1 1/2 teaspoons sugar

Preparation

In a small pan over medium heat sauté the garlic and shallots in the oil until fragrant. Add tamarind juice, oyster sauce, and sugar. Mix well. Remove from heat and
serve.

SPICY SATAY SAUCE

Ingredients

1 tablespoon soy sauce
8 shallots, sliced
8 garlic cloves, sliced
2 slices fresh galangal root (or 1 tablespoon galangal powder)
2 slices of fresh ginger
4 fresh chilies, seeded and sliced
1 tablespoon black pepper
1 tablespoon powered coriander
1 tablespoon fish sauce
2 tablespoons Palm sugar, brown sugar can also be used

Preparation

Combine all paste ingredients in a food processor. Push pulse a few times until the
ingredients turn into a paste. In a pan over medium heat sauté the paste briefly in hot
oil. Cool the spice mixture and rub over the meat cubes. Cover and let marinate in the
refrigerator for one to two hours.

PEANUT SAUCE

Ingredients

1/2 cup creamy peanut butter
1/4 cup red curry paste
2 cups coconut milk, don't sake the can before opening
1/4 cup sugar
1/4 cup tamarind juice
1/4 teaspoon salt

Preparation

Mix the peanut butter and red curry paste together well. Skim one cup of coconut cream from the surface of the coconut milk. Heat the coconut cream in a wok over medium heat until the oil surfaces. Be careful to keep stirring otherwise the milk will curdle as the temperature approaches boiling point. Add the peanut butter-curry paste mixture and stir well. Add the remaining coconut milk and reduce the heat. Continue to stir for 10 minutes. Add sugar, tamarind juice and salt to taste. Pour into a bowl and serve.

FISH HOT SAUCE

Ingredients

1 tablespoon fish sauce
2 tablespoons lime juice
1 teaspoon sugar
6 fresh chilies, sliced
3 stalks cilantro, chopped
2 shallots thinly sliced

Preparation

Combine fish sauce, lime juice, sugar, chilies, cilantro, and shallots together in a bowl. Mix well and serve.

CLAY BAKED FISH SAUCE

Ingredients

2 tablespoons fish sauce
1 tablespoon lime juice
1 tablespoon seeded and chopped fresh chilies
1 teaspoon cilantro, chopped
1 clove garlic, chopped

Preparation

In a small bowl combine all the ingredients and serve with Clay Baked Fish fish.

ORANGE MUSTARD SAUCE

Ingredients

1/4 teaspoon dry mustard
2 tablespoons orange juice
1 tablespoon lemon juice
1 teaspoon sugar
1/2 teaspoon salt
1 tablespoon chopped cilantro
1/2 teaspoon Tabasco sauce

Preparation

Combine all sauce ingredients in a bowl and mix well.

CHICKEN HOT SAUCE

Ingredients

2 tablespoons Sriracha hot chili sauce*
1 tablespoon fish sauce
1 tablespoon sugar
1 clove garlic, crushed

Preparation

In a small bowl combine all sauce ingredients. Mix well and serve.

* Sriracha hot chili sauce is made from chilies, vinegar, garlic, salt and sugar. You should be able to find it in Asian markets that sell Thai and Vietnamese imported foods. Sriracha is the brand name of such a sauce made in Thailand. Rooster brand is from Vietnam.

GARLIC SAUCE

Ingredients

4 slices white bread, trimmed and soaked in water for 10 mins.
6 cloves garlic, minced
2 tablespoons lime juice
1 tablespoon sesame oil
1/2 teaspoon salt
4 fresh chilies, seeded and chopped
2 tablespoons fresh cilantro, chopped
1–2 tablespoons water

Preparation

Remove bread from water, squeeze out excess liquid and place into a food processor. Add garlic and lime juice and blend. With the processor running, add sesame oil, salt, and fresh chilies. Blend until smooth. If the mixture is too thick or dry add small amounts of water until the consistency is correct for dipping. Pour the sauce into a bowl. Stir in cilantro by hand and serve.

SPICY DILL SAUCE

Ingredients

1/2 tablespoon oil
1 clove garlic, chopped
1 cup chicken broth
1/2 teaspoon salt
2–4 fresh chilies, sliced
1/2 tablespoon fish sauce
2 tablespoons lime juice
1 tablespoon cornstarch
3 tablespoons fresh dill, snipped from stem

Preparation

In a saucepan heat the oil over medium heat. Add garlic and sauté briefly. Add chicken broth, salt, chilies, fish sauce, lime juice, and cornstarch. Bring the mixture to a boil stirring constantly until mixture thickens. Boil 1 minute. Stir in dill.

SOY BEAN GINGER SAUCE

Ingredients

3 tablespoons yellow soybean paste
1 teaspoon dark soy sauce
1 tablespoon vinegar
1 teaspoon sugar
1 teaspoon fresh ginger, minced
1 clove garlic, minced
2 fresh chilies, seeded and smashed

Preparation

Combine all ingredients in a bowl. Mix well and serve.

FERMENTED SOY BEAN SAUCE

Ingredients

3 tablespoons fermented soy beans
1 tablespoon dark soy sauce
1 tablespoon vinegar
1 teaspoon sugar
1 tablespoon grated ginger
1 chili, thinly sliced

Preparation

In a food processor blend all ingredients to a paste. Spoon into a serving bowl and serve.

SWEET CHILI SAUCE

Ingredients

1 tablespoon red chili powder
1/2 cup vinegar
1 teaspoon salt
2 tablespoons sugar
1 tablespoon chopped garlic

Preparation

Mix all ingredients in a small saucepan over medium heat and bring to a boil, stir-ring constantly. Heat until sauce reaches a syrupy consistency. Remove from heat and serve.

SWEET CHILI PEANUT SAUCE

Ingredients

1/3 cup vinegar
2 tablespoons sugar
1 teaspoon salt
1/4 cup sliced shallots
1 red chili, thinly sliced
1/2 cup peanuts, freshly roasted and ground

Preparation

Heat the vinegar, sugar, salt, shallots and chilies stirring constantly until sugar dis-solves. When the mixture comes to a boil remove from heat. Pour into a serving bowl. Mix in ground peanuts and serve.

GREEN CURRY HEARTS OF PALM WITH MEKONG CATFISH

CURRY PASTES

Most of you will not have the time or the inclination to prepare your own curry pastes. But I wanted you to know what the ingredients are for the various curry pastes. It is not difficult to make your own and the fresher the better. Even today most cooks will make the paste in small quantities using a mortar and pestle. The purists swear they taste better made that way. You can use a blender or a food processor to hasten the job. And it sure does make the kitchen smell great.

There are many good curry pastes on the market now. The pastes that come in a can tend to be better than any of the powdered ones. Both the ones you make and the ones you buy can be stored in a sealed glass jar in the refrigerator for about 3 to 4 months.

ROASTED CHILI PASTE
RED CURRY PASTE
GREEN CURRY PASTE
YELLOW CURRY PASTE
SOUR CURRY PASTE
KAENG KHUA CURRY PASTE
MASSAMAN CURRY PASTE

NAM PRIK PHAO
ROASTED CHILI PASTE

Ingredients

2 cups vegetable oil
8 shallots, sliced
6 garlic cloves, sliced
1 cup dried shrimp
1/2 cup small dried chilies
1 tablespoon palm sugar
2 tablespoons fish sauce
1 1/2 tablespoons tamarind juice
1/3 teaspoon salt

Preparation

Heat the oil in a wok and fry the shallots and garlic until golden brown. Remove from oil and drain. Add the dried shrimp and dried chilies to the hot oil and fry until brown. Remove from oil and drain. Using a mortar and pestle or blender grind the shrimp, garlic, chilies, shallots and sugar until smooth. Add the fish sauce, tamarind juice, salt, and cooled oil from the wok to the blender. Blend until you have a finely textured paste.

NAM PRIK KAENG DAENG
RED CURRY PASTE

Ingredients

1 tablespoon coriander seeds
1 teaspoon cumin seeds
13 small dried chilies, soaked in hot water for 15 minutes and seeded
3 tablespoons chopped shallots
4 tablespoons chopped garlic
1 tablespoon chopped galangal
2 tablespoons chopped lemon grass
2 teaspoons chopped kaffir lime rind
1 tablespoon chopped coriander root
20 black pepper corns
1 teaspoon shrimp paste

Preparation

In a wok over low heat dry fry the coriander seeds and cumin seeds for about 5 minutes. Grind into a powder. Put the rest of the ingredients, except shrimp paste, into a blender and blend to a paste. Add the coriander–cumin powder and the shrimp paste and blend until smooth.

NAM PRIK KAENG SOM
SOUR CURRY PASTE

Ingredients

7 dried chilies, soaked in hot water for 15 minutes and seeded
3 tablespoons chopped shallots
1 tablespoon chopped garlic
2 tablespoons chopped krachai
1 tablespoon shrimp paste
1 tablespoon salt

Preparation

Put all the ingredients, except shrimp paste, into a blender and blend to a paste. Add the shrimp paste and blend until smooth.

NAM PRIK KAENG KARI
YELLOW CURRY PASTE

Ingredients

1 tablespoon coriander seeds
1 teaspoon cumin seeds
3 tablespoons chopped shallots
1 teaspoon minced fresh ginger
4 tablespoons chopped garlic
2 tablespoons chopped lemon grass
1 teaspoon salt
2 teaspoons shrimp paste
2 tablespoons yellow curry powder
3 dried chilies, soaked in hot water for 15 minutes and seeded

Preparation

In a wok over low heat dry fry the coriander seeds, cumin seeds, shallots, ginger and garlic for about 5 minutes. Grind into a powder. Put the rest of the ingredients, except shrimp paste, into a blender and blend to a paste. Add the powdered ingre-dients and the shrimp paste and blend until smooth.

NAM PRIK KAENG KHUA
KAENG KHUA CURRY PASTE

Ingredients

5 dried chilies, soaked in hot water for 15 minutes and seeded
3 tablespoons chopped shallots
2 tablespoons chopped garlic
1 teaspoon chopped galangal
1 tablespoons chopped lemon grass
1 teaspoon chopped kaffir lime rind
1 teaspoon chopped coriander root
2 teaspoons salt
2 teaspoons shrimp paste

Preparation

Put all ingredients, except shrimp paste, into a blender and blend to a paste. Add the powdered ingredients and the shrimp paste and blend until smooth.

NAM PRIK KAENG KHIAO WAN
Green Curry Paste

Ingredients

15 fresh green hot chilies
3 tablespoons chopped shallots
1 tablespoons chopped garlic
1 tablespoon chopped galangal
1 tablespoon chopped lemon grass
1/2 teaspoon chopped kaffir lime rind
1 tablespoon chopped coriander root
5 black pepper corns
1 tablespoon coriander seeds
1 teaspoon cumin seeds
1 teaspoon salt
1 teaspoon shrimp paste

Preparation

In a wok over low heat dry fry the coriander seeds and cumin seeds for about 5 minutes. Grind into a powder. Put the rest of the ingredients, except shrimp paste, into a blender and blend to a paste. Add the coriander-cumin powder and the shrimp paste and blend until smooth.

NAM PRIK KAENG MASSAMAN
MASSAMAN Curry Paste

Ingredients

3 dried chilies, deseeded and soaked in hot water for 15 minutes
3 tablespoons chopped shallots
2 tablespoons chopped garlic
1 teaspoon chopped galangal
1 1/4 tablespoons chopped lemon grass
2 cloves
1 tablespoon coriander seeds
1 teaspoon cumin seeds
5 pepper corns
1 teaspoon salt
1 teaspoon shrimp paste

Preparation

In a wok over low heat dry fry the coriander seeds and cumin seeds for about 5 minutes. Grind into a powder. Put the rest of the ingredients, except shrimp paste, into a blender and blend to a paste. Add the coriander–cumin powder and the shrimp paste and blend until smooth.

CUSTARD IN A PUMPKIN

DESSERTS

Because our traditional kitchen is not set up with an oven for baking, cakes and pastry are not a part of Lao food culture. The most popular dessert is fresh fruit. When we do cook a dessert it is either boiled or steamed.

YOUNG COCONUT ICE CREAM
PASSION FRUIT COCONUT ICE CREAM
LYCHEE WHIP
LYCHEE SHAKE
BANANA IN COCONUT MILK
BANANA CHIPS
MELON IN COCONUT MILK
CUSTARD IN A PUMPKIN
SWEET STICKY RICE WITH MANGO
STEAMED RICE CAKE with SWEET POTATO
STEAMED STICKY RICE IN A BANANA LEAF
STICKY RICE COOKED IN GREEN BAMBOO
VIENTIANE MANGO FOOL

ITEAM MAPLAU OUNE
YOUNG COCONUT ICE CREAM

Coconut ice cream is a big hit with children everywhere, anytime.

Ingredients

3 cups of half and half
1 (14 oz) can condensed milk
1 cup sugar
2 fresh young coconuts, discard juice and thinly slice the meat
Or 2 cans of young coconut meat

Preparation

In an ice cream freezer container combine all ingredients. Mix well. Freeze according to manufacture's instruction.

Makes 1 1/2 quarts

ITEAM MAKNOOD
PASSION FRUIT COCONUT ICE CREAM

This recipe contains uncooked egg yolks for those of you who should not eat uncooked egg yolks. The best passion fruit comes from the north of Laos.

Ingredients

8 passion fruits
2 cups coconut milk
2 egg yolks
2 tablespoons honey
A touch of salt
4 tablespoons sugar

Preparation

Cut the passion fruit in half. Scoop out all center pulp into a mixing bowl. Reserve 4 tablespoons for garnish. Add coconut milk and egg yolks to the passion fruit pulp and mix well. Add sugar, honey, and salt. Continue beating until well mixed. Pour the passion fruit mixture into a shallow container and freeze for 1 hour. Remove mixture from the freezer and beat with a fork until it forms a smooth slush. Return to the freezer and freeze until completely firm. Remove the ice cream from the freezer 5 minutes before serving. Pile scoops of ice cream into stem glasses and garnish with the reserved passion fruit pulp.

Serves 4

LAMYAI WOON
LYCHEE WHIP

Few fruits can rival a sweet and juicy fresh lychee nut. Unfortunately, fresh lychees start losing their sweetness after being picked. In the West, we are more familiar with the canned variety. Fresh, frozen lychees are available now in most Asian markets.

Ingredients

3/4 cup of boiling water
1 package Jell-O any flavor (4 serving size
1/2 cup of cold water
2 cups of ice cubes
1 cup of fresh* or canned lychees fruit
Fresh mint for garnish

Preparation

In a mixing bowl combine boiling water with Jell-O. Pour into a blender. Cover and blend at low speed until Jell-O is completely dissolved. Add cold water and ice cubes, mix until ice is partially melted. Blend at high speed for 30 seconds. Pour into dessert glasses or serving bowls. Spoon lychees over the top (reserve a little lychee, sliced, for garnish). Chill until firm, 20 to 30 minutes. Dessert layers as it chills. Garnish with remaining sliced lychees and mint if desired.

* If using fresh lychee fruit remove the seeds first.

Serves 8

LAMYAI PAN
LYCHEE SHAKE

Lychees grow wild in many parts of Laos and Thailand. Lychee recipes for both sweet and savory dishes abound.

Ingredients

1 can lychees or 1 lb. of fresh lychees, remove seeds and slice
2 cups milk
1/2 cup sugar
Mint for garnish

Preparation

Combine lychees, milk and sugar in a blender. Blend at high speed until smooth. Serve with mint leaf garnish.

Serves 4

KUAY BUAD
BANANA IN COCONUT MILK

This rich concoction is originally a famous Vietnamese dessert, but it is now a favorite on any local Lao menu. A scoop of ice cream is perfect with this dessert.

Ingredients

4 ripe bananas
4 cups of fresh coconut milk
1/2 cup of palm sugar
A pinch of salt

Preparation

Peel bananas and slice into one inch to one and a half-inch lengths. Steam for 15 minutes and set aside. In a large pot combine coconut milk, palm sugar, and a pinch of salt. Place over high heat and bring to a boil. Reduce the heat to simmer. Add bananas, and cook for 1 hour. Pour into individual serving bowls to cool. Can be served hot or cold.

Serves 6

KAUY KOB
BANANA CHIPS

These banana chips are very crispy. An excellent beer snack they are also delicious served with coffee or tea.

Ingredients

4 firm green bananas
1 cup lime juice
4 cups oil for deep-frying
1 cup sugar

Preparation

Peel and thinly slice bananas. Soak in lime juice for 10 to 15 minutes. Rinse and drain well. Heat oil to 375 F. and deep-fry banana slices until golden brown and crispy. Drain on paper towels. In a saucepan melt the sugar over high heat. Stirring the melted sugar continue to cook until syrupy and golden brown. Gently pour the melted sugar over banana chips, turning carefully.

Serves 4

TEANG MO NAMSEOUM
MELON IN COCONUT MILK

Boiled coconut milk with palm sugar and, just about anything makes a refreshing dessert. Be inventive; try palm seeds or flavored gelatin. These desserts can be served either warm or cold.

Ingredients

15 small honeydew melon balls
15 small Watermelon balls
2 cups fresh coconut milk
A pinch of salt
1/2 cup palm sugar or white sugar

Preparation

Set aside 3 to 4 tablespoons of the coconut milk. In a small pan heat the remaining coconut milk over a medium to high heat. Stirring carefully, bring the coconut milk to a boil. Add the sugar and salt. Continue boiling, stirring constantly until sugar is melted. Pour into a bowl and refrigerate. After mixture has chilled combine with the melon balls. Top with the reserved coconut milk and serve.

Serves 4

SANG KAYA MA EUD
CUSTARD IN A PUMPKIN

You want to find a small pumpkin for this dessert. If it is not the season for pumpkin, you can use a small kabocha squash. Sometimes called Thai squash or Japanese squash, kabocha is a small, round squash with firm flesh.

Ingredients

4 eggs
1/4 cup coconut milk
8 tablespoons palm sugar or white sugar
A pinch of salt
2 tablespoons shredded fresh coconut meat (optional, for garnish)
1 small Pumpkin or kabocha squash

Preparation

Cut the top off the pumpkin and remove seeds. Rinse well and dry the inside with a paper towel. In mixing bowl combine eggs, coconut milk, sugar, and salt. Vigorously beat until sugar dissolves. Pour into the pumpkin and steam on a steaming rack for 45 minutes. Check to make sure the eggs have set. Remove from the steamer and refrigerate. After pumpkin is cooled cut into triangular pieces, top with the fresh, shredded coconut and serve.

Serves 4

KAONEO MAMAUNG
SWEET STICKY RICE WITH MANGO

Lao people love mangos and sticky rice. So do Thais, for that matter. We love them green. We love them ripe. We love them sweet. We love them sour and bitter. We even love them green with hot chili powder and salt. During mango season different kinds of mango and sticky rice concoctions are served from street stalls and at local fairs on holidays.

Ingredients

1 cup steamed sticky rice
1 cup fresh or canned coconut milk
1 teaspoon salt
1/2 cup palm sugar or white sugar
1 to 2 fresh, sweet mangoes, peeled and sliced

Preparation

Heat the coconut milk in a pan with salt and sugar, bringing it to a boil. Reserve 4 tablespoons of the coconut milk mixture for garnish. Add the sticky rice to the pan stirring constantly to prevent the rice from sticking to the sides. Continue stirring until the liquid is gone. Place rice mixture in a bowl to cool. Separate into 4 portions and place on small plates with the sliced mango. Top with reserved sweet coconut milk and serve.

Serves 4

KA NOON NEAB
STEAMED RICE CAKE with SWEET POTATO

This "rice cake" is like Japanese mochi, rather than what we think of as a rice cake. There are endless variations on this dessert theme. Use your imagination. Use lotus paste or black sesame paste instead of the sweet potato for example.

Rice cake ingredients

3 cups coconut milk
1/2 cup palm sugar or white sugar
1 1/2 cups sticky rice flour
1/2 cup regular rice flour
A pinch of salt
1 eight-inch square banana leaf
Sesame oil, to oil banana leaf

Stuffing Ingredients

1 cup steamed sweet potato, mashed
1/2 cup palm sugar or white sugar

Rice cake preparation

In a medium size saucepan, heat the coconut milk. Add sugar, stirring well to dissolve. Continue stirring and slowly add the sticky rice flour. Add the regular rice flour and the salt, stirring all the while. When the mixture is very sticky remove to a bowl to cool.

Place the piece of banana leaf in a bamboo steamer tray. Wipe a light layer of sesame oil on top of the banana leaf to prevent rice balls from sticking.

Stuffing preparation

Combine the mashed sweet potato with the sugar.

Place 1 tablespoon of rice mixture in your hand and roll it into a small ball. Form an indentation in each ball and place about a teaspoon of the sweet potato inside the hole. Squeeze the top of the hole together to seal in the sweet potato trying to maintain the round shape.

After re-shaping each of the rice balls, place them on top of the banana leaf in the steamer tray. Steam for 15 minutes.

Serves 6

KAO TOM PAT
STEAMED STICKY RICE IN A BANANA LEAF

I guess we Lao would be lost for dessert ideas if we didn't like sticky rice. Since I grew up eating sticky rice I have no idea if it really is as good as I think it is or if it is an acquired taste.

Ingredients

3 cups sticky rice
4 cups coconut milk
1 cup sugar
2 teaspoons salt
4 bananas, quartered to make 16 sections
16 Banana leaves, cut to 6" x 7" pieces
16 rubber bands or lengths of twin to secure rice bundle

Preparation

In a saucepan, combine the coconut milk and the uncooked sticky rice. Bring slowly to a boil, stirring occasionally to keep the rice from sticking to the bottom of the pan. Continue boiling and stirring until all of the coconut milk has been absorbed. Add a small amount of water. Continue stirring and cooking until rice is done. Add sugar and salt, stirring well to dissolve. Remove saucepan from heat to cool.

Wrapping instructions

Place 1 1/2 tablespoons of the cooked sticky rice in the center of a piece of banana leaf. Place one section of banana alongside the sticky rice and mold the rice around the banana. Add sufficient sticky rice to the other side of the banana to enclose it. Fold the banana leaf around the mixture and secure with a rubber band or string. Put the bundles into a steamer tray and steam for 20 minutes.

Serves 6

KAO LAM
STICKY RICE COOKED IN GREEN BAMBOO

When I cook this dish at my home, I use purple sticky rice in this recipe. If you can find purple sticky rice in your market use it. If you cannot find it, then white sticky rice will do.

Ingredients

2 sections of young, green bamboo*
2 cups sticky rice, soaked in water 2 hours
1 cup taro root, cut into small pieces
2 tablespoons sugar
A pinch of salt
4 cups coconut milk
2 pieces of fresh banana leaf, for stuffing into bamboo
wood or charcoal for grilling

Preparation

Wash and drain the rice. Mix rice, taro root, sugar, salt, and coconut milk together in a bowl. Spoon the mixture into the young bamboo sections. Seal with a banana leaf by wadding the green leaf and stuffing it into the open end of the bamboo section. Grill the Bamboo-rice 30 to 45 minutes and let it cool. Check to see that the rice is cooked before serving. If the rice is not thoroughly cooked steam for 20 minutes and serve. Gently smash the bamboo cylinder and peel off the strips before serving.

* Each green bamboo section should be about 12 inches long and 3 to 4 inches in diameter. Cut so that only one end is open.

Serves 2

MAMOUNG JOXE
VIENTIANE MANGO FOOL

To cool the palate after a spicy Lao meal, the taste of mango, lime, ginger and coconut cream is perfect.

Ingredients

3 ripe mangoes
1 slice fresh ginger, shredded
1 cup powered sugar
1 tablespoon lime juice
1/2 cup of heavy cream
1/2 cup of coconut milk
A pinch of salt

Preparation

Cut mangoes in half. Cut and reserve 2 slices for garnish. Scoop out the remaining pulp into a bowl. In a food processor or blender combine the mango pulp with the ginger, sugar, lime juice, coconut milk, and salt. Puree in the blender or food processor until smooth. In a mixing bowl whip the cream until soft peaks form, fold into the mango puree using a large spoon or rubber spatula. Divide the mixture into 6 portions and pour into serving glasses. Refrigerate for at least 1 hour before serving. Cut the reserved mango slices into 12 smaller slices. Decorate each desert with the small slices of mango and a sprinkle of powered sugar.

Serves 6

FRESH COCONUT MILK

GLOSSARY

Ant Eggs, frozen ones are available in many Thai and Vietnamese markets. The best eggs come from the ants that live on the mango and logan trees. The tree ant builds large nests that hang under the branches of the tree. To gather the eggs, which are shaped like small peanuts, knock the nest into a bucket of water held underneath the branch. The recently hatched ants float on the surface of the water. Scoop them off and discard them.

Anchovy Paste is a greyish, thick paste made by grinding salted and fermented anchovies. Thicker than fish sauce it is used as a seasoning in everything from soup stock to stir-fried meats and vegetables. Its popularity extends from Thailand to the Philippines.

Bamboo Shoots are, along with soy beans, some of the most versatile and useful plants in Asia, where they originated. The crunchy texture and slightly acidic flavor of bamboo shoots make a unique addition to innumerable dishes. One eats the fresh young shoots available in spring and winter. Fresh bamboo shoots contain a toxin that can be gotten rid of by blanching for 5 minutes. Rinse well before using. Canned ones are readily available in most markets as well as pickled ones. There are actually three kinds of bamboo that are eaten in Laos; *no mai lai (Gigantochlea Nigrociliata), no mai bong (Bambusa Tulda)*, and *no mai hok (Dendrocalamus Hamiltonii)*.

Banana, *Nam Wa* variety, *kluai nam wa*, (sometimes known as apple bananas), *Musa Sapientum*, is probably the most popular eating banana among the nearly thirty varieties found in Laos. It has short oblong fruits that become a pale yellow as they ripen. The leaf, *bai tong*, of this variety is used in the recipe Steamed Sticky Rice in a Banana Leaf.

Banana Leaves are available fresh or frozen in many Asian markets these days. Wrapping goes more easily if the sections are torn and allowed to stand overnight before wrapping. The larger leaves from fresh collard greens make a good substitute if you don't have any luck finding fresh banana leaves.

Basil. There are many types of basil. The most commonly used basil in Lao cooking is sweet basil, *horapha*. It has deep green leaves and often reddish or purple stems. It has a taste reminiscent of anise and is especially good in curries. If you can not find *horapha*, any basil can be substituted. *Maeng lak* is another sweet basil with light green leaves and a tangy taste.

Bean Curd is made from soybeans that are soaked, ground, mixed with water and briefly cooked before being placed in a wooden mold to drain and solidify. There are several types of bean curd. Different types of dishes and different methods of cooking call for different types of bean curd. Soft white bean curd, tau hoo, is most often steamed or added to soups while the firm type, tao kwa, is used for stir-frying, deep frying and braising. Refrigerated bean curd will keep for about five days if the water is changed daily. Pressed and deep fried bean curd is also available. It can be found in dried cakes in most Asian markets.

Bean Curd, fermented, *tau hoo yee*, is more like cheese than tofu. It can be eaten with rice, used in cooking to enrich vegetable dishes or used as a seasoning. The two most common types are red fermented bean curd and white fermented bean curd. The red variety is cured in brine with fermented red rice flavored with annatto seeds and rice wine.

Bean Curd, Spongy. Deep-frying bean curd changes the texture into a sponge-like substance. This allows the bean curd to absorb the flavors of the sauce when it is cooked for a second time.

Bean Sauce, a seasoning made from fermented soybeans, flour and salt. This very popular Asian seasoning appears as yellow bean sauce, brown bean sauce, black bean sauce and hot bean sauce. The preferred sauce is made from whole beans, as the ground varieties are often quite salty.

Beans, Black Fermented, also known as salted black beans, are cooked and fermented with salt and spices. These small, black, salted soy beans have a fantastic flavor when combined with garlic, fresh ginger, or chilies. Some chefs soak the beans before use; others use them directly from the container, crushing or chopping lightly to release the aroma.

Beans, Mung, *thua khiao*, are yellow beans with green shells. The shelled bean is used in sweets and the whole bean is sprouted, giving bean sprouts, *thua ngok*.

Beans, Yard-Long, thua fak yao, have pods up to 60 cm long. These are eaten both raw and cooked and are at their best when young and slender.

Cabbage, Chinese, *phak kat khao, Brassica Campestris (Pekinensis* variety), has thin, light green leaves and broad, flat, thin ribs which form an elongated, rather than a spherical, head.

Celery, Chinese, kheun chai, Apium graveolens, also called celeriac, turniprooted celery , has very small stalks and a very strong flavor.

Chicken Stock, *nam sup*, made from fresh chicken is preferred in Lao cooking. While plain water can be substituted and the instant chicken broth cubes and pastes are certainly fast and convenient, they do not compare to home made stock. Chop 3 1/2 pounds of chicken bones and scraps into 3-4 inch pieces and place in a stockpot with 10 cups of water and allow to stand for 30 minutes. Peel 1 Chinese radish, cut in half length-wise and add to pot. Wash 3 Chinese celery plants and 3 garlic plants and remove the roots of the celery plants. Coil the celery and garlic plants together, tie into a bundle and add to the pot together with 5 bay leaves and 1 tablespoon salt. Heat to boiling, simmer over low heat for 1 to 1 1/2 hours and then strain through cheesecloth.

Chilies, Hot, *Capsicum Frutescens*, several varieties are available in Laos. As they ripen they change color from green to red and become hotter. Removing the seeds and pulp from fresh chilies reduces their hotness. Fully ripe fruits are dried in the sun to give dried chilies, *mak phet haeng* and these are pounded for ground dried chili, *mak phet pun. Mak phet dip* refer to fresh chilies, still green. *Mak phet deng* are fresh chilies after they turn red. *Mak phet nyai* are large chilies and mak phet kuntsi, are the smallest (and also the hottest) of the elongated chilies, being only about a centimeter long. The smallest chili is called *mak phet kinou* (rat droppings chili). Generally the smaller the chili the hotter the flavor. *Capsicum Annum*, is what we know as the bell pepper, sweet pepper or pimento. It is used in stir-fried dishes and makes a great receptacle for almost any type of stuffing. It is not nearly as important as hot chilies in Laotian cooking.

Chili Sauce, *phed saus*, is made from water, chilies, salt, vinegar and sugar. The taste and degree of hotness or sweetness varies according to the brand. Many different brands from most Asian countries are available. Sriracha is a very popular Thai brand of chili sauce.

Chili Paste, see curry paste section after Dipping Sauce section in main text of *Taste of Laos*.

Chinese Chives, ton kui chai, Allium tuberosum, has fairly thick, narrow flat leaves which are eaten with fried noodle dishes such as Pad Thai.

Cilantro (see coriander)

Coconut Milk, *ka-thi* is the white liquid that is squeezed from grated coconut meat and not the juice inside the coconut. The use of coconut milk in curries is a hallmark of both Lao and Thai cooking. To prepare about 1 1/2 cups coconut milk, add 2 cups fresh grated coconut to a food processor or blender. Add 1 1/4 cups very hot water and blend at high speed for one minute. Strain mixture through a fine sieve, pressing hard with a wooden spoon to extract as much liquid as possible. This is coconut milk. For recipes calling for thick coconut milk, allow the coconut milk to stand for a while, the thick milk will rise to the top. Spoon it off the top. This is coconut cream. The left over liquid will be light coconut milk. When cooking with coconut cream, be careful to keep stirring otherwise the milk will curdle as the temperature approaches boiling point. To prepare coconut milk from dried coconut flakes empty an 8-ounce package of unsweetened dried coconut flakes into a food processor. Add 2 cups of very hot, near boiling, water. Process with quick on and off pulses for 25 seconds or until well mixed. Strain the mixture through a fine sieve, pressing hard with a wooden spoon to extract as much liquid as possible. Canned coconut milk is very convenient and quite good. If a recipe calls for thick coconut milk, open the can and remove the thick milk that rises to the top. Use the contents just below the thick milk in recipes that call for light coconut milk. When the recipe calls for coconut milk, shake the can before opening.

Coriander, *phak chi, Coriandrum Sativum,* is a member of the parsley family. The leaves (referred to as cilantro in the text) and stems are eaten fresh and used frequently as a garnish. The root and the seeds are ingredients in many dishes. The root is taken from the fresh plant. The seeds, which are roughly spherical and range in color from off-white to brown, have a pleasant taste and fragrance. It is better to roast and grind seeds immediately before use than to buy ground coriander seeds.

Cucumber, Asian, *taeng kwa,* has short fruits about 8 cm long which are crispiest while still green and white, before yellowing. A larger type, taeng ran is also eaten.

Cumin, *yi ra, Cuminium Cyminum,* has elongated yellow-brown seeds about 5 mm in length. They should be dry roasted before use to heighten their fragrance.

Curry Powder, *phong ka ri,* is a prepared mixture of spices such as turmeric, coriander seeds, ginger, cloves, cinnamon, mustard, cardamom, cumin, chili and salt. Each brand has its own character depending on the ingredients used.

Curry Paste, See curry paste section after Dipping Sauce section in main text of *Taste of Laos.*

Dill, *Anethum Graveolens,* most often used in fish dishes is *phak shee* in Lao. Alan Davidson writes that the dill in Laos is the same species as in Europe and the Near East but different from the dill of India and Indonesia, *Anethum Sowa.*

Ear Fungus, *het hu nu,* is a dark grayish brown fungus that has a delightful crunchy texture. Soak in hot water for about 15 minutes and rinse well before use.

Eggplant, *ma kheua, Solanum Spp.* In Lao cooking there are several types of eggplant aside from the more common long, thin lavender Chinese eggplant or the smaller nearly black Japanese eggplant. *Ma kheua yao* tastes very similar to Chinese and Japanese eggplant except they are green. These are served grilled, broiled or in curries. *Ma kheua phuang, Solanum Torvum,* grow in clusters and look like large peas. These miniature eggplants are slightly bitter but they nicely offset the rich taste of the curries in which they are used. *Ma kheua pro* is about the size of a ping pong ball. They can be white with a green cap, yellow-orange or purple in color. This eggplant is often eaten raw with a dipping sauce, or slightly cooked in salads or curries.

Fiddle Head Fern, is the young coiled frond of various species of ferns eaten as vegetables. Pick the young tightly coiled fronds.

Fish Sauce, *nam pa*, is a clear brown liquid derived from a brew of fish or shrimp mixed with salt. It is sold in bottles and plastic jugs as well as in earthenware jars. High quality fish sauce has a fine aroma and taste. Fish sauce is placed on the table as a condiment at nearly every meal either as is or mixed with sliced chilies and perhaps lime juice. In Thailand it is called *nam pla*; in Vietnam, *nuoc nam*; in Burma, *ngan pya ye* and in Cambodia, *tuk trey*.

Galangal, *kha, Alpinia Galangal*, is a larger and lighter colored relative of ginger and has its own distinctive flavor.

Garlic, *kra–thiam, Allium Sativum*, is used both by the clove and by the entire bulb. The dry papery skin and the central core should be removed from bulbs. Cloves are often crushed by hitting with a spatula or the side of a knife blade and then the skins are picked out. Pickled garlic, kra–thiam dong, are wonderfully flavorful and can be bought by the bulb or by the jar in the market. Set on the table at mealtime it is a popular accompaniment to steamed rice.

Ginger, *khing, Zingiber Officinale*, grows from an underground stem, or rhizome. Mature ginger stems are buff colored. Young or fresh ginger, khing on, is white and is eaten fresh and pickled as well as cooked. It is also a popular accompaniment to steamed rice. It is also useful as a remedy for motion sickness and upset stomach.

Kaffir Lime, *mak khi hiut, Citrus Hystrix*, has green fruits with wrinkled skin. The rind and leaves are used in Lao cooking. In Thailand it is *ma–krut*.

Krachai, *Kaempferia Panduratum*, sometimes known as lesser galangal grows in bunches of slender and short yellowish brown tuberous roots and is most often used in fish dishes.

Lemon Grass, *sik hai, Cymbopogon Citratus*, is an aromatic green grass. It is closely related to citronella grass. The bases of the stems are used in cooking. The fresher the plant the more of the stem you can use. Older plants are more fibrous. When using older plants you should peel off a few of the outer layers before using. The outer layers of the stalk can be used to make tea. As a medicinal agent, lemon grass is good digestion. It is called ta–khrai in Thai.

Logan, *lam–yai*, is smaller than a lychee and has a smooth, thin yellowish–brown skin. The flesh is similar in color to the lychee but not quite so sweet or juicey. Logan grow in bunches on farily large trees.

Lychee or Lychee Nuts, originated in Southern China. It resembles a small golf ball covered in a reddish, rusty, leather–like skin and a large black seed. The almost translucent flesh is sweet and juicy. Fresh lychees are a special treat indeed. Only a fresh, juicy mangosteen can rival the sweetness of a good quality lychee.

Mackerel, *pa thu*, is a small salt water fish, *Rastrelliger Chrysozonus (Scombridae)*. Steamed mackerel in small woven trays are sold in food shops nearly everywhere in the country.

Mango, of which there are many varieties are more readily available in spring through early summer. Some mango skins turn yellow or red when ripe others remain green after ripening. Green mango does not mean simply a mango with a green skin but an unripe one. The mango is a member of the cashew family and is one of he most popular fruits in Southeast Asia.

Mango, Green, are hard unripe mangoes often eaten raw with salt and chilies. Also used in salads and sauces and made into pickles.

Mangosteen, in season between December and February, is a plump persimmon shaped fruit with four green leaves on top. The sweet, segmented, white flesh is encased in a dark purple, fibrous shell.

Mungbeans, *thua khiao*, are yellow beans with green shells. The shelled bean is used in sweets and the whole bean is sprouted, giving bean sprouts, thua ngok.

Mushrooms, Cloud Ear's, see Ear Fungus.

Mushrooms, Oyster, is delicately flavored with a faint oyster aroma. They come in clusters and have large, wide, fluted caps. Its color ranges from gray to beige.

Mushrooms, Shiitake, *hed hom, Lentinus Edodes*, often called Japanese dried mushrooms. The Japanese cultivate them on the shii tree, thus the name *shiitake*, (*take* is Japanese for mushroom). The Chinese have been gathering them for over a thousand years and prefer them dried to fresh. The best tasting and most expensive mushrooms are the large, thick light brown ones with a cracked surface, but all grades add flavor and aroma to any recipe.

Mushrooms, Straw, *het fang*, used in soups, salads and curries. Straw mushrooms have a sweet and nutty flavor and although they are available canned we suggest you substitute a fresh alternative such as oyster mushrooms.

Mustard Greens, Chinese, *phak kwang tung, Brassica Campestris (Chinensis* variety), has dark oval leaves on thick fleshy stalks.

Noodles, Egg, *ba mi*, are yellow noodles made from wheat flour and eggs. Small balls of this kind of noodle are available in the market.

Noodles, Mungbean, wun sen, are thread-like noodles made from mung bean flour. They are sold dried and are soaked in water before use. When cooked they become transparent. High quality noodles maintain their integrity in soup better than do cheap ones.

Noodles, Rice, *kuai-tiao*, are flat white noodles made from rice flour. Uncut fresh noodle sheets are sold in the market. They are also sold in three widths: wide, sen yai (2–3 cm), narrow, sen lek (5 mm) and thin, sen mi (1–2 mm). Dried noodles are soaked in water before use to soften them.

Noodles, Vermicelli, *khanom jin*, are thin round noodles, made from either wheat or rice flour. Fresh vermicelli is sold in the form of wads that look like birds nests.

Ong Choi, see water spinach

Onion, *hom hua yai, Allium Cepa*, has light colored bulbs that are larger and milder that those of the shallot.

Onions, Spring, *ton hom, Allium Fistulosum*, also called spring onions or scallions, has leaves that are circular in cross section. These are much used as a garnish. The bulbs are frequently served on the side of one-dish meals, such as fried rice, or placed on a salad plate.

Oyster Sauce, *nam man hoi*, is a rich, viscous seasoning sauce made from fresh oysters, salt and spices. A wonderful and popular seasoning for seafood, meat and poultry. It is especially good over stir-fried vegetables such as *kai lan, bok choi* and *choi sam*.

Padek, a variant of the ubiquitous Southeast Asian fish sauces (*nam pla* in Thailand, *nuoc mam* in Vietnam) is a rough product containing bits of fish and rice husks; it has a powerful smell, so the large earthenware pot containing it is usually stored outside the house. It is specific to Laos and the Lao-inhabited territories of northern Thailand, and its frequent use as an ingredient in Lao dishes helps to make them distinctive.

Palm Sugar, *nam tan pep*, was originally made from the sap of the sugar Palmyra palm, Borassus flabellifera, which has a very rough trunk and large, fan-shaped leaves. Now it is generally made from the sap of the coconut palms and may be sold as coconut sugar. The sugar is a light golden brown paste with a distinctive flavor and fragrance.

Prawns, Dried, *kung haeng*, are small shrimp which have been dried in the sun. Look for the bright orange ones, as they are the best. Dried shrimps should be soaked in hot water or rice wine before use. The soaking liquid can also be used.

Radish, Chinese, *hua phak, hus chai hao, Raphanus Sativus, (Longpinnatus* variety), has a long, cylindrical root that looks like a hefty, white carrot.

Radish, Preserved, sometimes called salted turnip, is available in Asian markets. It should be washed before use. It is another popular Asian accompaniment to steamed rice.

Rice, *khao jao*, the staple food in the central and southern parts of Thailand, is long-grained, non-glutinous rice. Uncooked grains are translucent. When cooked, the rice is white and fluffy.

Rice, Crispy. Packages of crispy rice cakes are available in most Asian markets. Toasted and crumbled it adds a wonderful crunch to salads.

Rice, Fermented, *khao niao*, is made by fermenting cooked glutinous rice and is sold as a sweet.

Rice, Glutinous, *khao niao*, also known as sticky rice, is the mainstay of the diet in Laos and the northern and northeastern regions of Thailand and is used in confections in all regions. Uncooked grains are starchy white in color.

Rice, Sticky, see rice, glutinous.

Rice Flour, *paeng khao jao*, is made from non-glutinous rice.

Rice Flour, Glutinous, *paeng khao niao*, is made from glutinous rice.

Rice Paper, made from a mixture of rice flour, water and salt. Rice paper needs to be softened before use. Carefully dip one or two sheets in a warm sugar-water solution and soak until soft, a minute or two. Drain on a towel before rolling. Look for white rice papers. Stay away from packages with broken pieces and yellowish papers.

Rice Powder, Roasted. Roast a small amount of rice in the oven until completely dried. Grind into a powder. Roasted rice powder should be kept in an airtight jar until needed.

Rice Wine, brewed from glutinous rice. Use Chinese *Shaoxing* rice wine for the recipes in this book (A good, dry pale sherry can be substituted). Japanese rice wine, sake, is quite different and should not be used.

Roasted Sticky Rice Powder. Roast a small amount of sticky rice in the oven until completely dried. Grind into a powder. Roasted rice powder should be kept in an airtight jar until needed.

Rock Cod, *pa kao*, is also known as grouper, reef cod, and sea bass.

Sea Perch, *pa ka phong*, is a general name for fish of the sea bass and sea perch families.

Sesame, *nga, Sasamum Indium*, has small oval seeds that are white and have dark hulls. They are usually sold hulled.

Shallots, *hom lek* or *hom daeng, Allium Ascalonicum*, is the zesty small red onion favored in Lao cooking.

Shrimp Paste, *ka-pi*, is shrimp which is salted, fermented for a time, allowed to dry in the sun then ground and worked with the addition of moisture into a fine-textured paste, which is fragrant and slightly salty. A little bit goes a long way for the Western palate.

Soy Sauce, *si iu*, used in these recipes is the Chinese rather than the Japanese type. Soy sauce is prepared from a mixture of soybeans, flour and water, which is fermented and aged. The three most commonly used soy sauces are light soy sauce (*si iu khao*), dark soy sauce (*si iu dam*) and mushroom soy sauce. Light soy sauce can be substituted as a vegetarian alternative to fish sauce. Dark soy sauce is aged longer than light soy sauce and is slightly thicker, sweeter and stronger although light soy sauce is usually saltier. The dark soy sauce is preferable for dipping while the light soy sauce is most often used in cooking. Mushroom soy sauce is infused with straw mushrooms and imparts a delicious flavor.

Sponge Gourd, *buap liam, Luffa Acutangula*, also called *Angles Luffa*, vegetable gourd, silk squash, or Chinese okra, is oblong, pointed, and dark green and has sharp longitudinal ridges. Peel away the tough ridges and slice crosswise. If it is older it is best to peel away the skin. If younger you can leave on some of the green skin. When cooked it absorbs the flavors in which it is cooked, thus the name sponge gourd.

Sugar, *nam tan sai*, is granulated cane sugar. Colors range from white to reddish and textures from fine to coarse. Some people find the reddish sugar tastier than the more highly refined white.

Tamarind, *ma-kham, Tamarindus Indicus*, is a tree which bears tan pods inside of which are bean-like hard brown seeds surrounded by sticky flesh. The tan pod shell can be easily removed. Ripe tamarind, *ma-kham piak*, is the flesh, seeds, and veins, of several fruits pressed together in the hand to form a wad. The immature fruit, the young leaves and the flowers are also used, all to give a sour taste. Dried tamarind pods as well as pressed pulp is available in most Asian markets. If you can't find tamarind you can substitute lime or lemon juice sweetened with a little brown sugar. Should you ever encounter a hooded cobra and it spits its lethal venom into you eye, wash the eye with juice squeezed from fresh tamarind leaves. If you can't find any tamarind leaves lime juice will do

Tamarind Juice, *nam som ma-kham*, is obtained by mixing some of the ripe fruit with water and squeezing out the juice. Jars of tamarind juice are available in most Asian markets.

Tapioca Pellets, *sa-khu met lek*, are tiny balls (about 2 mm in diameter) made from tapioca (cassava tubers), used in some sweets. They should be mixed with hot, but not scalding, water and kneaded, and allowed to stand for a time covered with a damp cloth to permit the water to penetrate to the core.

Tapioca Flour, *paeng man sampalang*, is made from tapioca, or cassava tubers. When this or any of other flour is used to thicken a sauce it is first mixed with a little water so it will not lump in the sauce.

Tofu, see bean curd.

Turmeric, *kha–min, Curcuma Longa,* is a small ginger with brown rhizomes. Inside the flesh is a bright carrot orange. Also used as a coloring agent. Be careful it does not wash off the hands easily.

Water Spinach, *phak bung, Ipomoea Aquatica,* also called water convolvulus, swamp cabbage, or aquatic morning glory, has hollow stems and roughly triangular leaves. The Lao variety has delicate dark, green leaves and deep red stalks while the Chinese variety, ong choi, is thicker, larger, and lighter green. The tender tips of the stems are eaten fresh or cooked.

Wax Gourd, *fak khiao, Benincasa Hispida,* also called white gourd or Chinese preserving melon, is oblong and light green to white. The ends are rounded and the flesh is solid and white.

Won Ton Skins, it is no longer necessary to make these by hand. Very good commercially made wrappers are available at most markets. Buy the very thin ones if possible. They freeze very well, so you can use what you need and wrap the unused wrappers well before freezing.

INDEX

133

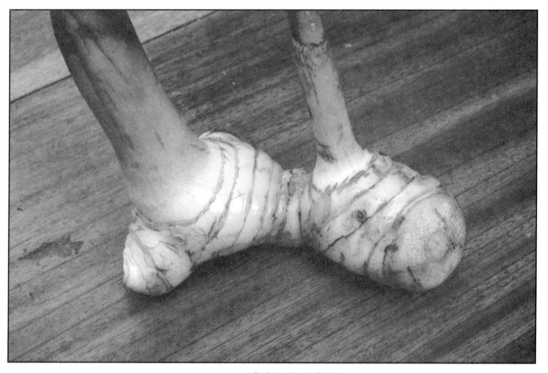

GALANGAL

MA KHEUA PRO EGGPLANT

KAFFIR LIME LEAVES

MA KHEUA PHUANG EGGPLANT